THE MACRO FAIRE

AN INVESTOR'S GUIDE TO MACROECONOMICS

ANKITA PATHAK

ISBN 979-8-89026-925-6

Editing Credits: Machinga LLP

Contents

Acknowledgement

The idea of writing a book wouldn't have taken shape in my mind had my colleague *Sahil Kapoor* not inculcated an aggressive reading and writing habit in me, which has changed my life in many ways! I owe a whole lot of my knowledge to him. I'd like to thank my beloved mother *Sushma* for instilling in me the spirit of living up to my full potential. She has magnified my ambitions through her infinite prayers. Lastly, I'd like to express heartfelt gratitude to my partner-in-everything, *Manas*: you're the wind beneath my wings.

Introduction

"It is no crime to be ignorant of economics, which is, after all, a specialised discipline and one that most people consider to be a 'dismal science.' But it is totally irresponsible to have a loud and vociferous opinion on economic subjects while remaining in this state of ignorance."

– Murray N. Rothbard,
American economist and political theorist

My reason for writing this book can be summed up as an extension of the quote above: if you're an investor, it can likely be unprofitable to have an incomplete or unclear view of certain key macroeconomic ideas.

It's true that economics in general is highly vulnerable to the risk of being too detached from reality. The real world is too messy and interlinked to be captured by a handful of equations. Cycles are similar, but never the same. Despite that, macroeconomics is essential in order to develop accurate views regarding the markets and various asset classes, and to determine a logical asset allocation scheme.

It was sheer luck that led to me starting my career as an economist in the Indian capital markets. The only active role I played in this situation was a firm resolve to return to India from the UK after graduating, and to then understand and serve India. Early on, I was convinced that typical textbook theses had a lot of value, but it soon dawned on me that most of them hadn't been tailored for an economy like India's. And even on the rare occasions when some such thesis was in fact tailored to India, it wasn't applicable to capital markets.

After having spent seven years in institutional equity management, wealth management, and asset management in India, I felt it was time to fill in the gap and talk about the macroeconomic indicators that matter for the Indian markets. This book focuses on theory, the real meaning of various indicators, how they are created in the first place, and how they're applied to yield a top-down view of asset classes. It aims to make it easier for you to understand and track these indicators. However, the caveat indicated above remains true: no relation discussed in these pages is a truth cast in stone, because economics is an art as well as a science, meaning that nuanced human judgement is always indispensable.

Close to a hundred macro data points get released every month. They vary in terms of the frequency of their release and the period of data capture. For example, inflation data released in March will show the actual inflation of February, but the Index of Industrial Production (IIP) data released in March shows the actual data for January. All this data can feel overwhelming, and is either ignored or overemphasised. And this data almost always sparks the question: will it have an effect on the markets tomorrow?

On the one hand, everyone's excited to have some means of predicting, even if only crudely, what's going to happen in the markets. On the other hand, they typically end up scratching their heads as to why the markets aren't reflecting the latest data. My base case is that macro data does influence markets, but there are several caveats to be borne in mind. First, markets are forward-looking, which means they make moves even before the associated data is released. In other words, macro data lags behind the markets, which move based on expectations rather than actual releases. It's possible for a market to hit a lifetime high on a day when the real GDP is announced to be extremely low. Why? Because the market has already priced in the assumption that the worst is behind it, and that future data is likely to be better.

Second, surprises delivered by data affect markets, not the data itself. For instance, if the market's expectation was that the central bank will increase interest rates, but the latter holds them steady instead, then this is considered a dovish move, and both equity and debt markets will react positively. However, if the expectation was that of a pause and the policy does indeed deliver a pause, then this is effectively a non-event. Most of the seeming dichotomy between macro data and the markets can be explained by the forward-looking nature of the markets and their tendency to react only to surprises.

The same data can yield different insights. While data is quantitative, insights are qualitative. A given piece of data can speak very differently to you and me, and that's okay. For instance, a credit growth of X% might excite person 'A', but person 'B' might dismiss the trend saying, "This growth is mainly driven by medium and small industries, which have disproportionate benefits at this juncture". Or person 'A' might fret about high inflation, but person 'B' might consider it to be a completely harmless variable in the cycle.

In addition, there are different temporal ways of analysing data, such as Year-on-Year (YoY) or Month-on-Month (MoM), which measure the current data against data from a year or a month before, respectively. There are additional complications as well, such as base effects, sampling errors, etc. There are also many different solutions to such issues, such as taking longer-term CAGR to adjust for base effects, adjusting samples for like-to-like comparison, and so on. The many problems and many solutions make understanding these indicators interesting. Only when there is an asymmetry in conclusions is there a decent likelihood of rewards.

This book dives deep into several economic indicators that can add value to investors. The approach taken here is more practical rather than theoretical. The best part is probably that it's tailored to the Indian context. Towards the end, this book presents the big picture, the real world as seen from 30,000 feet up, along with its many nuances. It's beautiful, it's chaotic, and it's exhilarating. It's about how A usually leads to B, but how this time around C is more powerful, and therefore A may lead to less of B and more of D. Understanding why A usually leads to B and, more importantly, what A and B actually are, is the crux of this book. The applications of the ideas it presents are many. But know that it doesn't come with ready-made answers. It's only a toolkit: you're the one with the exciting task of applying it!

Chapter 1

Inflation: Painful But Necessary

In late 1324 CE, the inhabitants of Cairo were a happy lot: on the whole, they had all suddenly become wealthier! Over the next few years, however, their joy would be steadily replaced by despair and frustration, as their economy started to fray at the seams.

And all this due to the generosity of a man who might have been the richest person to have ever lived.

For it was in 1324 CE that Mansa Musa, the then ruler of the Mali empire (which spanned a large swath of land in Western Africa, including parts of modern-day Mali, Guinea, Senegal, Mauritania, and The Gambia), set forth for Mecca to perform the obligatory hajj. The Mali empire had become unfathomably wealthy as a result of gold and salt mining, as well as due to its participation in the slave and ivory trade. Despite all its wealth, however, it was not very well-known to the world at large. Musa decided to make use of his hajj not only to assure his soul a place in heaven but also to assure his country a place in historians' chronicles. And it worked: this pilgrimage literally put the Mali empire on the map, as it began appearing in cartographers' works soon after.

Musa headed to the holiest city of Islam with an almost brazenly large entourage that was meant to drop jaws and evoke awe: he took with him 60,000 people, of whom 12,000 were slaves entrusted to carry 1.8 kg of gold bars each (that's more than 20,000 kg of gold!). There were also 80 camels carrying several tens of kilos of gold dust. It's said Musa had a mosque built every Friday, and freely handed out gold to poor people he met along the way.

This massive caravan reached Cairo in July, 1324 CE. Musa sojourned in Cairo for three months before continuing on his way to Mecca. During this stay, he reputedly introduced so much gold into the city that the Egyptian economy ended up crashing, with prices of goods and services soaring: such a scenario is now called inflation, and will be the focus of the rest of this chapter.

Now, there's actually a fair bit to unpack here. It might not be very apparent why more gold circulating among a region's inhabitants should lead to such a painful state of affairs, where people have to cough up ever more money to feed, clothe, and house their families (a pain that's undoubtedly very relevant even today). So let's try and break down this complex maelstrom of economic cause and effect into more manageable and more local interactions, so that we can see how the additional gold injected into Cairo might have made more mundane necessities more expensive.

Let's say it's been a week since Musa began handing gold out and buying souvenirs and trinkets at whatever price sellers quoted. How might the market dynamics have changed?

For starters, the price of gold will have gone down. There are two main reasons for this. One is that psychologically, we tend to desire scarce things more than easily available things. The influx of gold into the system will have made gold less scarce, thus diminishing its value in our eyes, and hence the price we're willing to pay for it (in general, the price we're willing to pay for something can be seen as a proxy for the value we ascribe to that thing).

The other reason is that there will probably be more potential sellers in the gold market now, which means increased competition among gold sellers. Now, one of the simplest ways to gain a competitive advantage is to reduce your prices. This reduces your profit margin, sure, but you hope to make up for that by selling larger volumes.

Taken together, these two reasons will have caused the price of gold to drop. But gold would still be valuable, and anyone who had simply been given some gold by

Musa would definitely be a much wealthier person. And over time, through the buying and selling of goods and services, this gold would get distributed among more and more people.

So Musa's generosity has introduced fresh money (very broadly speaking) into the Cairene economy. Why will the prices of everyday goods go up as a result? Let's make it even simpler: why should potatoes become more expensive as a result?

To understand this, let's zoom in on a small and ordinary Cairene market, called the Souk ul-Ma'aqool (or just 'the Souk' for short). The Souk has several potato sellers. Now, it's possible that the prices of potatoes might go up simply because the sellers all banded together and decided to charge more, knowing that most of their customers had additional cash to spare. However, this is not a very common way for prices to rise in the real world: in actuality, things are usually more organic. Here's one way potato prices could have gone up organically in this situation.

Let's say all of the potato sellers in the Souk try to sell their wares until 6 pm every day. Most days are good, but sometimes, some sellers might have some unsold stock left at the end of the day. Now, one week after Musa's arrival in Cairo, all of the potato sellers have begun selling out their entire stock by 3 pm. Why? Well, the average person has more money now, so the total number of potential potato buyers has gone up, as has the average number of potatoes each person is able to buy.

So most of the potato sellers are happy that they're getting some extra leisure time, and start enjoying long siestas after 3 pm. But one of the potato sellers, a young upstart named Aladdin, decides to take a small risk and try something new: he raises his prices just a little bit.

What do you think will happen? Well, if the price increase is low enough, then given the fact that there's plenty of demand for potatoes, and given the fact that all the other sellers are running out of potatoes by 3 pm, it's possible that Aladdin manages to fully sell his stock only by 6 pm. But this means that he's still working the hours he was before, but is now getting more money for doing so. From his point of view, this is absolutely worth doing.

And this won't escape the notice of his fellow sellers, of course. They'll soon realise what's happening, and will also want to get in on the action. And soon, once everyone's raised their prices, the average price of a potato in the Souk will be higher than what it used to be before Musa and his gold came along.

This kind of scenario can be generalised to many everyday goods and services. For certain other kinds of goods and services, such as luxury goods or housing, the mere fact that the average buyer/renter now has more money to spend can enable sellers to raise their prices and rents without any negative repercussions. And this is how Cairo (and eventually Egypt as a whole) ended up experiencing, in the wake of Musa's stay there, a continuous general increase in the prices of goods and services, i.e. inflation!

Now, at this point, it's important to clarify that this popular story is a hybrid of history and hyperbole (as tantalising stories usually are), and that it's been argued that the decrease in the price of gold resulting from Musa's generosity was in fact within normal limits. Nevertheless, it makes for a fascinating and edifying framework within which to understand the basics of inflation, so we'll go along with the hyperbole for now.

The most important takeaway of this story is probably the general correspondence between scarcity and value: the less available something is, the more we tend to value it, and vice versa. Thus, ultimately, if inflation involves a general price rise, this means that one of the following (or a combination) must be true:

- Certain goods and services are becoming scarcer
- The demand for certain goods and services is becoming higher,
- Money itself is becoming less scarce, due to which we value it less and are more willing to part with it.

The Basics Of Inflation

Inflation is probably the most well-known macroeconomic indicator since most people are at least vaguely familiar with it. You'll sometimes find it being described as "a necessary evil", "a wealth destroyer", and other expressions in that vein. The concept is simple enough: inflation measures changes in prices. So when your parents tell you that an outing at a restaurant used to cost no more than INR 40, but that anything less than INR 1000 is pretty much unthinkable today, what they're really rueing is inflation. When you start to grumble at the prices of fruits, vegetables, tea, coffee, chocolate, and various other consumables, what you're unhappy about is inflation.

There are two main drivers of inflation: high demand and low supply. In the high-demand scenario, the "demand pull" leads to relatively lower availability of goods/services(for same supply, the demand is much higher), making them scarcer and thus more expensive. For instance, after the worst of the Covid-19 pandemic was over and China had reopened, it was feared that the demand for commodities would rise so fast that the existing supply would not be enough, leading to demand-pull inflation. This kind of inflation usually happens when an economy is doing well in terms of growth. It can also be a consequence of high income levels, as seen in the wake of the unemployment cheques disbursed in the US during the pandemic.

The second main driver of inflation is low supply, or a "supply squeeze". During the Covid-19 pandemic, the production of various kinds of goods came to a halt, leading to limited availability and a sharp rise in their prices. This kind of inflation is also known as "cost-push" inflation. China is also a major producer of commodities and semi-conductors, and China shutting down led to a supply squeeze during the pandemic. Similarly, inflation typically shoots up during and after wars as equipment and capital is destroyed and production along with supply chain is hampered. Soon after the Russia-Ukraine war had started, the expectation of a reduced supply of oil from Russia caused oil prices to go up.

Two Key Indices

India mainly measures two types of inflation:

1. Consumer Price Index (CPI) inflation: CPI inflation is a measure of typical retail inflation, the one you and I feel when we buy the final goods. The price of my chocolate going up is captured in CPI inflation.

2. Wholesale Price Index (WPI) inflation: this measures the price spikes seen by wholesalers, e.g. the cost of milk and cocoa powder going up for chocolate producers. In the rest of the world, this measure is typically called the Producer Price Index (PPI).

For both of these types, there's something known as "core" inflation, i.e, inflation without accounting for growth in food and fuel prices. This is the true representation of domestic prices. Why exclude food and fuel prices, though?

The first reason is that they're volatile. The second is that they're influenced by factors beyond what domestic policymakers can control. For instance, both food and fuel prices are governed by global demand and supply. The RBI increasing interest rates can't bring down the price of Brent crude oil. Therefore, central banks focus more on core inflation, i.e, the structural inflation in the economy after removing the cyclicity and volatility.

The CPI inflation figure usually gets announced on the 12th of every month, while the WPI inflation one gets announced on the 14th of every month. For instance, on the 12th of December, we get the actual CPI figure for November, and on the 14th of December we get the actual WPI figure for November. Of course, if there's a public holiday on the scheduled dates, the dates are adjusted to the next working day. The main difference between these two inflation types is in the baskets(components) and calculation methodologies for these inflation figures.

Before we go any further, we should understand something called 'base setting'. What is a base? Like in mathematics, a base year is a year where the relevant inflation index is set to 100. Then, for every incremental year, the growth in index is calculated. If the index for

2012 is set at 100 and the index goes up to 110 in 2013, newspaper headlines will flash a reading of 10% inflation in 2013.

Every few years, the MOSPI (Ministry of Statistics and programme implementation) revises the base of the inflation basket. Why? Because consumers' consumption habits evolve. For instance, a relatively old base for measuring CPI inflation established that 23% of a consumer's expenditure goes into services such as personal care, health expenses, transport, and communication, etc. However, as per the 2012 base, 28% of average consumer expenditure goes towards these services. Share of entertainment and recreation in our overall consumption budget has gone up. So has our need to dine out on weekends or travel every few months. Today, food basket is overweight on 'cereals' especially 'wheat and rice'. In future, can millets be more important part of food consumption budget of India? Possibly, yes.

As an economy evolves and develops, the nature of consumption moves from necessities to luxuries. Expenditure on food decreases and that on travel and tourism goes up. If people are gymming more and consuming more health supplements, the weight of these components in the overall inflation basket should increase. Thus, the base is revised to better reflect the consumption patterns of the economy. However, past and present data cease to be comparable when the base is revised because the methodology and the inherent composition of the basket change.

This issue can be addressed by making use of a technique called "vertical spliced series", which creates hypothetical past data based on the current methodology and basket. This is slightly more complex a topic but for those of us are interested, full methodology is available on the MOSPI website.

The current baskets for the CPI and WPI are as follows:

CPI Components	Weight (%)
CPI	**100**
Food, beverages, and tobacco	**46**
i. Cereals and products	10
ii. Milk and products	7
iii. Vegetables	6
iv. Oils and fats	4
v. Meat and fish	4
Fuel and light	**7**
Housing	**10**
Clothing, bedding, and footwear	**7**
Miscellaneous	**28**
i. Transport and communication	9
ii. Medical care	6
iii. Education, stationery, etc.	4
iv. Personal care and effects	4
v. Household requisites	4
vi. Recreation and amusement	2

WPI Components	Weight (%)
Primary articles	**23**
i.　　Food articles	15
ii.　　Non-food articles	4
iii.　　Minerals	1
iv.　　Crude petroleum and natural gas	2
Fuel and power	**13**
i.　　Coal	2
ii.　　Mineral oils	8
iii.　　Electricity	3
Manufactured products	**64**

**Rounded down to the nearest whole number*

Source: MOSPI

The difference between the compositions of their baskets is clearly a major differentiator between the two types of inflation. While food is a major contributor to the CPI basket, the WPI basket places a lot of emphasis on commodities. Hence, there are times when the CPI and WPI inflation figures are very different.

When inflation is driven by food prices, the CPI rises much faster. When commodity prices shoot up, the WPI rises much faster. The gap between the WPI and CPI is important from the markets' perspective too. When the WPI is going up but the CPI is not, it means that the inflation faced by wholesalers is rising, but they're unable to pass that inflation on to end consumers, possibly because the demand for their goods is weak. As a consequence, in such a situation, wholesalers' margins will shrink. This can be extrapolated for the economy as a whole, and data shows that a growing gap between the WPI and the CPI leads to lower margins for companies, and vice versa.

Now that we have a reasonably good understanding of the CPI and WPI, let's see how inflation interacts with various markets.

Inflation And Financial Markets

Central banks have a mandate to ensure relative price stability while also managing growth. They use interest rates (i.e. the repo rate in India or the federal funds rate in the US) as a tool to try and tweak inflation levels. When inflation rises, central banks raise interest rates. Why? Well, higher interest rates lead to more expensive credit, and thus lower demand. They also reduce the amount of money available in the economy. This leads to a curbing of inflation expectations, and ultimately a reduction in the inflation rate itself. Indeed, inflation expectations play a huge role in the RBI's judgements, as policymakers and consumers act on inflation expectations. These expectations are measured directly via the central bank's surveys.

Once the inflation rate has fallen, central banks can keep rates constant for a while or reduce them to fuel the economy and maintain a target inflation rate (India aims to maintain inflation at around 4%, with a deviation of two percentage points in either direction being considered acceptable).

Let's start with bonds. Lower inflation means lower interest rates by central banks. While we'll delve deeper into why this is the case in the chapter on monetary policy, for now, what's important to know is that central banks try to maintain price stability. Lower inflation means interest rates can be lowered to spurt demand and get inflation closer to the target. Bond yields are directly linked to RBI's interest rates. Therefore, lower inflation translates to lower bond yields.

Now, a bond's yield is its coupon (interest payments) divided by bond's price. Hence, the lower the yield, the higher the bond's price, as the coupon usually remains fixed for the tenure of the bond. A bond's duration is indicative of how much its price is likely to change when interest rates move. Therefore, a long-duration bond will see a higher increase in price for a given decrease in bond yields. Hence, investing in long-duration bonds when inflation is falling can be a good idea, as investors will make capital gains on the bonds with an increase in bond prices.

There are two types of premiums that bonds command on top of benchmark interest rates: a time premium and a risk premium. Long-term bonds have higher yields than RBI's benchmark interest rate because of the higher time the lender needs to be invested in them. If the repo rate is 6% and the 10-year yield of G-Secs ('government securities', i.e. bonds issued by a government) is 7%, the time premium is 100 bps (100 bps = 1 percentage point). The risk premium, on the other hand, is the excess yield over the risk-free sovereign (i.e. G-sec) rate that non-sovereign entities pay because there's a risk of default. For example, a company might borrow at 10%, i.e. with a risk premium of 300 bps (3% higher than the sovereign yield of 7%).

Thus, in sum, bond market yields are mostly linked to the benchmark interest rates set by the central bank. However, depending on the nature of a bond — its risk profile and maturity — the yield premium it commands can continue going up.

As mentioned above, lower inflation leads to lower yields and higher capital appreciation on long-dated bonds. When inflation is rising and consequently interest rates are also rising, it makes sense to consider investing in short-duration bonds. This is because raising of interest rate by central banks will first transmit towards the shorter duration bonds. Thus, in a rate cut cycle, longer duration bonds are likely to be favourable and in rate hike cycle, shorter duration bonds make more sense.

Let's move on to the equity markets now. In this context, inflation is both a pain and a perk. Let's consider the points that matter to decide here-

a. When inflation goes up, the top-line revenue of companies starts to increase. Therefore, for the same volume of sales, the value of revenue looks higher. For instance, if a company sold N units for INR 1, its top-line revenue will be INR N, but if it sells N units for INR 1.25 in the next year, its top-line revenue will jump to INR 1.25N, a jump of 25% without any change in volume.

b. So higher inflation can lead to higher revenue. However, equity markets care about earnings or profits and those are adjusted for the costs. Whether or not the cost of raw materials has gone up by the same magnitude is industry dependent. If it has, then the net effect of this situation on company profits will be determined by the difference between the revenue increase and cost increase.

c. It makes sense for investors to study every industry and invest in sectors for which the increase in revenue is higher than increase in costs when inflation is high. For example, auto companies use metals as raw material, when price of metals go up, their margins are hit but if the demand in economy is strong, they can pass on the input cost to the final consumer and conserve their margins and profitability.

d. Market valuations correct themselves as interest rates go up in a rising inflation scenario; this reduces the current value of future earnings. It also increases the cost of capital for companies and could weigh upon their profitability

In a falling inflation scenario, the same cost vs revenue price differential needs to be calculated to determine which sectors will benefit. For the market as a whole, valuations tend to inch higher, because future earnings look brighter as lower inflation is accompanied with lower interest rates. For instance, the NIFTY 50 was trading at a 32X P/E multiple in 2020, thanks to a record-low interest rate of 4%.

Clearly, the interaction between inflation and the equity markets has a fair number of nuances to it. As a thumb rule, a moderate to moderately high inflation rate (in India's context: 4-6%) is good for the equity markets. An overly low inflation rate is a sign of low growth, depressed earnings, and overpriced valuations. An excessively high inflation rate affects the final demand and kills producer margins, as the cost of raw materials also goes up.

As far as currency is concerned, high inflation causes the home currency to depreciate, ceteris paribus (i.e. all other things being the same). However, when it comes to the home currency's exchange rate with a different country's currency, then the inflation differential for the two countries needs to be studied: the absolute values don't have much relevance here. INR/USD pair will therefore be affected by relative inflation differential in the two economies.

Lastly, as far as commodities are concerned, it's my opinion that changes in commodity prices are themselves expressions of inflation. In other words, changes in commodity prices and inflation are inextricably associated with each other, and move more or less in tandem. Commodity prices are important constituents of the inflation basket.

Inflation And Purchasing Power

Friday night. Karan has just entered a multiplex with his work friends, and makes a beeline for the food area: he has a bit of a weakness for sugar. He asks for a chocolate doughnut, and is surprised to learn that he needs to pay INR 90 for it. That's because he remembers that the last time he'd bought one of those doughnuts a month ago, he'd only paid INR 80. Oh well, the price is the price. He shrugs, pays up, and catches up with his friends.

Saturday morning. Despite his penchant for sweets, Karan's typical diet is very healthy, so he steps out to pick up some fruits and vegetables from the market nearby. But today, he raises his eyebrows every time a seller quotes him a price. When did bananas and lemons get so expensive, he wonders.

Sunday afternoon. Karan gets a call from his landlord informing him that from the next month onwards, he'll have to pay 10% more rent. Karan's quite displeased about this. The landlord couldn't care less.

Monday evening. Karan's annual appraisal has gone well, and he's stoked to learn his employer wants to offer him a raise: the rent hike will pinch less, he figures. But then it turns out that his pay will only go up 5%.

The last thing Karan feels that night before sleep overcomes him is dejection at the prospect of losing more money every month.

Karan's experience of coming face to face with the seemingly ugly reality of inflation is probably quite a common one, because inflation definitely has a way of creeping up on you. It affects your purchasing power. But while this phenomenon holds several negative connotations in the minds of laypeople (and probably rightly so), it is also true that a controlled amount of inflation enables economies to keep growing at a steady, sustainable pace. As for the erosion of real wealth that it causes, the best way to combat it is probably to understand its effects on various financial market instruments and then make wise investment decisions accordingly. After all, sometimes, investing is all about beating inflation.

Chapter 2

Growth: All That Matters!

Seen broadly, the story of humanity is one of development, advancement, and progress, or to put it more succinctly, of growth. Stone tools gave way to metal instruments, tribes of hunter-gatherers gave way to settlements built around agriculture, and humility in the face of the natural world has given way to a zeal for taming the hardships Mother Earth throws at us.

But at smaller timescales, say over a few years or decades, the picture can be obstinately hazy: it can be impossible to figure out whether a given society is growing or not, at what rate, and in what ways. And not having answers can mean being rudderless: if you don't know if something's wrong, how can you even begin to fix it?

That's exactly the predicament in which the US government found itself during what we now call the Great Depression: things certainly seemed bleak, sure, but how bad was it really? Was it just a temporary panic that would soon fade away, or was it the kind of situation that would require major government intervention to remedy? But no one had any real answers to these questions.

Eventually, an economist and statistician named Simon Kuznets was charged with leading a team that would gather useful information about the state of the American economy. The 261-page report that his team submitted in 1934 was ground-breaking: it calculated a value for the "national income and product", a metric that would soon be referred to as the Gross National Product (GNP). The GNP eventually morphed into the now-ubiquitous Gross Domestic Product, which countries around the world use to measure the state of their respective economies.

As economic historian Dirk Philipsen puts it in his book 'The Little Big Number: How GDP Came to Rule the World and What to Do About It':

"*It is no exaggeration to say that today, the entire world economy follows the basic script first drafted in this 1934 report.*"

GDP In The Indian Context

Projecting growth is almost always the be-all and end-all of economic analysis. Simply knowing what kind of growth one can expect from an economy can help answer many pertinent economic questions, such as where we are in the business cycle, what the sectoral growth rate is, which economy is relatively outperforming others, and so on. However, when it comes to growth rates in India, the big catch is that they become available only after a two-month lag.

For instance, the growth rate for the Jan-Mar quarter will only become publicly known on the last working day of May. As a result, in order to understand the economy in real time, it's now imperative to study high-frequency data. Many major agencies around the world have created models for "nowcasting" the GDPs of various countries; this is essentially based on crunching high-frequency data in such a manner that the output generated becomes a reasonable proxy for growth. In the near term, nowcasting does come reasonably close to the actual growth numbers. However, such models vary widely in terms of their robustness.

In this chapter, we'll analyse the customary publication of the growth rate and its various implications. Before we get started in earnest, however, remember that growth and the markets are never concurrent indicators: often, it's the markets that lead growth.

How The GDP Is Calculated

There are two main growth indicators in India: the Gross Domestic Product(GDP) and the Gross Value

Added (GVA). Technically, the GVA indicates an INR value for the amount of goods and services that have been produced in a country, minus the cost of all inputs and raw materials that are directly associated with that production. The GVA thus adjusts the GDP by taking into account the impact of subsidies and taxes (tariffs) on products. To use corporate terminology, the GDP is akin to total sales or total revenue, while the GVA is akin to net earnings.

Calculation of GDP by expenditure method clubs expenditure by different categories. The classic GDP equation is:

$$GDP = C + G + I + X$$

Which means that the output (GDP) is the sum of:

- Private consumption (C), which is what you, me, and other private consumers spend (think restaurant bills, wine bottles, expenditure on groceries, etc.),

- Government consumption (G), which is what the central and state governments spend (e.g. public schemes and possibly also the unlimited tea in government offices!),

- Investments in the economy (I) (roads, real estate, etc.), and

- The net exports (X), which are the total exports-total imports (with oil / luxury cars /engineering goods being examples of imports, and agricultural goods / services being examples of exports).

It should be noted that the first three components in the equation above add to the national output, which means they are all positive numbers. In contrast, the net exports take away from the national output, because India imports more than it exports, which means that this component is negative.

As of FY23, private consumption (C), referred to as Private Final Consumption Expenditure (PFCE) in the published GDP report, contributes ~58% to the GDP; government consumption (G), referred to as Government Final Consumption Expenditure (GFCE), contributes ~10%; and investments (I), referred to as Gross Capital Formation (GCF), contributes ~36%. Summing them brings us to ~104% of GDP: that's because net exports (X) takes away 3% of GDP, and another ~1% of GDP is taken away by discrepancies in the data collection methodologies.

The GVA, on the other hand, is measured by value addition in specific economic activities and is published along with an indication of key sectors. These sectors are self-explanatory: the three most important ones are agriculture, industry, and services, which are further divided into the following sub-sectors.

Component	% share in FY22
Total	100
Agriculture, forestry, and fishing	**16**
Crops, including irrigation	8
Crops	8
Irrigation	0
Livestock	5
Forestry and logging	1
Fishing and aquaculture	1
Industry	**31**
Mining and quarrying	2
Manufacturing	19
Food products, beverages, and tobacco	2
Textiles, apparel, and leather products	3
Metal products	3
Machinery and equipment	4
Other manufactured goods	7
Electricity, gas, water supply, and other utility services	2
Electricity	2
Gas	0
Water supply	0
Other utility services	0
Construction	8
Services	**53**
Trade, hotels, transport, and communication and broadcasting	18
Financial services, real estate, and professional services	22
Public administration, defence, and other services	13

Source: MOSPI

The reason for highlighting these components is to give you a fair idea of the kinds of components and the kinds of data you can expect to see in the official report. Now that we're aware of the outcome we expect from the GDP data, let's dive into some other nuances.

The GDP and GVA are published in two different forms, based on constant prices and current prices. To understand this, we need to revisit the concept of a base. A base year is a year for which prices are indexed as being 100 units, and any change in the output is calculated under the assumption that the price is still 100 units. Let me try to simplify this.

The current base year is FY12, which means that the prices in FY12 are taken to be 100 units. The GDP calculated using the FY12 base will assume that prices are still 100 units. Now, given that the output is the product of value and volume, this methodology captures the effect of the volume, because by assuming constant prices, it effectively assumes a constant value.

This is why the GDP calculated under the assumption of constant prices is also known as the 'real GDP', which is the nominal GDP minus inflation. The GDP in current prices (i.e. nominal GDP), on the other hand, calculates the output based on current prices, and therefore reflects the effect of both the value and the volume.

Let's look at a concrete example here. Assume that there are two chocolate bars in the economy in FY23: the price of each chocolate bar was INR 20 in FY12, but is INR 40 in FY23. In constant / real terms, the total value of the chocolate bars is INR 40, but in current / nominal terms, it is INR 80.

In the quarter that ended in March 2022, when the real GDP grew by a mere 4% due to the impact of the Omicron wave, the nominal GDP grew by 13% owing to the high inflation in the economy. This brings us to the concept of the GDP deflator. We have already seen that the GDP has many components, and each is adjusted based on the price that prevailed in the base year. On an aggregate basis, across all the goods and services of the economy, the measure of the price impact is called the GDP deflator. It is also referred to as the implicit price deflator because there's no direct way to calculate it.

However, here's a thumb rule from experience: the GDP deflator is roughly two-thirds of the wholesale price index (WPI) inflation and one-third of the consumer price index (CPI) inflation. Why? Because most of the categories in the GDP are affected by prices at the producer level, not at the consumer level.

Broadly speaking, the GDP is a compilation of data from many sources. As quoted in the Ministry of Statistics and Programme Implementation (MOSPI) methodology, "Broadly, the methodology for compiling the estimates of GDP consists in dividing the whole economy into various sectors comprising primary, secondary and tertiary activities. The estimates of GDP in respect of agriculture, forestry and logging, fishing, mining and quarrying, registered manufacturing (establishments registered under Factories Act, 1948) and construction are based on production approach. Income approach is used in the estimation of GDP originating in Un-registered manufacturing (establishments not registered under Factories Act), electricity, gas and water supply, trade, hotels and restaurants, transport, storage, communication, banking and insurance, real estate, ownership of dwellings, business services, public administration and defence and other services. The estimates of various services in the public sector are compiled by analysing the budget documents and annual reports of departmental and non-departmental commercial undertakings, those of the organised (registered) manufacturing sector are made using data from the Annual Survey of Industries, the estimates relating to the unorganised sectors in various economic activities are made using the figures of per worker value added available from the results of follow-up surveys of the Economic Census and the labour force in the activity. Generally, the unorganised sectors estimate of GDP is compiled for the base year or the bench mark survey year and estimates of subsequent years are obtained by moving the base year estimate with the help of appropriate physical indicators." For a deeper dive, visit https://www.mospi.gov.in/133-gross-domestic-product.

Thus, the GDP is the sum of the output of the different pillars of the economy. It brings together various kinds of sectors (organised and unorganised, listed and unlisted, formal and informal, etc.) under one umbrella through a rigorous methodology and helps us draw several useful conclusions. Many important indicators, such as debt, credit, current account balance, and trade balance, are typically studied as a percentage of GDP. This allows these indicators to be understood vis-a-vis the size of the economy. It also makes cross-country comparison possible. How else could one compare the US's indicators, which reflect an economy of USD 23 trillion, with India's indicators, which represent a USD 3 trillion economy?

More Specific Kinds Of GDP

There are two more GDP variants you should be aware of: GDP per capita and GDP by Purchasing Power Parity (PPP). The GDP per capita divides the total output by total population, and is supposed to indicate the material well-being of the populace, at least in theory. However, in practice, it's not the case that the entirety of the output is created by the people, nor is it attributed to the people. Some part of the output consists of corporate gains, while some is expenditure by the government on assets. Given India's vast population and income differential, it becomes difficult to draw many meaningful insights from this number.

As an aside, there's a theory related to GDP per capita that holds that when an economy starts to make more than USD 2,000 per capita, the GDP growth per capita accelerates significantly. India achieved this number in 2019. In that context, we are at the pivotal point of the J-curve and may grow rapidly in coming years.

The GDP by PPP (Purchasing Power Parity) is a method of calculating the GDP that takes into account the differences in the prices of goods and services in different countries. In other words, the GDP by PPP adjusts for the differences in the cost of living between countries, so that the GDP figures can be compared more accurately across countries. For instance, it takes into consideration the fact that a Starbucks coffee costs USD 1.3 in Turkey but USD 3.2 in the United States.

To calculate the GDP by PPP, the GDP of a country is first converted into a common currency, usually USD. Then, the prices of a basket of goods and services are compared across different countries, and adjustments are made to reflect the relative purchasing power of the currencies in each country. The resulting GDP by PPP figures provide a more accurate comparison of the relative economic activity and standards of living in different countries. Therefore, even though in absolute terms we are close to USD 3 trillion economy, in PPP terms we are close to USD 13 trillion and are the third largest economy globally, right behind US and China. The vast differential between two figures is because USD 1 has a higher purchasing power in India.

Common Terms In Business/ Economic Cycle

A **recession** is a period of temporary economic decline, typically lasting for at least six months, where there is a significant contraction in economic activity. During a recession, there are declines in GDP, employment, income, and trade. It is generally characterized by reduced consumer spending, business investment, and industrial production.

A **depression** refers to an extended period of severe economic contraction characterized by significant declines in economic activity, such as GDP, employment, and investment. Depressions are marked by their duration, depth, and widespread impact on various sectors of the economy. They are more severe and prolonged than recessions and often involve high unemployment rates, deflation, and financial instability.

Stagflation is an economic phenomenon characterized by a combination of stagnant economic growth, high unemployment, and high inflation. It is a situation where an economy experiences both a rise in price levels and a decline in output or economic activity. Stagflation is considered challenging to address because traditional policy tools that target either inflation or unemployment may have conflicting effects in this scenario. It can be caused by factors such as supply shocks, high energy prices, or other structural imbalances in the economy.

The **recovery** period is when these indicators start to improve, either through policy action or self-correcting mechanisms of the economy.

The GDP And The Markets

Without making this chapter any more technical or speaking of the drivers of growth(as are articulated in the Solow Model), I'd like to jump to the effects of the GDP for the markets. The number of connections between them are many, but are convoluted and mostly indirect. Moreover, they're all effective over a long term: in the short term, it's the markets that lead the economy. With those caveats out of the way, here's what we know.

A higher nominal GDP correlates with higher revenue growth of companies. Over a longer period, the overall corporate revenue growth rate converges with the nominal GDP. Needless to say, different sectors and companies have different growth rates. The sectors in the GVA could help here. When using a discounted cash flow (DCF) model for the broader markets, the nominal GDP serves as the most realistic measure of the terminal growth rate.

The real GDP helps us determine where we are in the business cycle. The gap between the RBI's estimate of the potential output and the published real GDP serves to determine the output gap which, along with inflation, forms the basis for the RBI's judgements on interest rates. Again, it should be kept in mind that interest rates affect both equity and bond markets. Investor sentiment is one of the factors that power the business cycle. Higher growth makes investor sentiment rosier, and bodes well for riskier assets. Higher growth also improves the rating of an economy, thus potentially attracting more inflows.

With all that said, let's now understand the effect GDP growth has on each asset class in isolation.

As far as currency is concerned, high growth is good for currency appreciation. A strong economy and higher interest rates are more likely to attract foreign investments, which can increase the demand for the local currency and cause it to appreciate against other currencies.

A relatively high GDP growth can also create demand-pull inflation. High, robust growth with high inflation leads to higher interest rates. This can lead to higher yields on bonds, as investors demand a higher compensation for the increased risk of inflation. Generally, yields on the longer end go up when growth or growth expectation is high, and come down when the economy is cooling off. For people investing in long-duration bonds, lower growth and inflation is beneficial as a fall in yields leads to a price rise. Small wonder, then, that during times of crisis, debt markets are where the most money is made!

For base metals, higher growth is good news as it indicates higher demand. This is relatively more dependent on economies that are major consumers of commodities, such as China. China's GDP and base metal demand / prices move more or less together. As commodities are priced in USD, the US's GDP is also significant. We look at these aspects much closely in the chapter on commdoties later. For now, it's important to know high global growth (especially that is driven by US and China) has proven positive for base metals. For gold investors, however, a lower growth regime is better. In such a regime, it is physical, risk-free assets that tend to outperform: recessions are generally associated with gold outperformance. However, when COVID-19 struck, central banks introduced so much liquidity that despite the sudden growth shock, it was the riskier assets that stood out.

Lastly, for equity investors, higher growth is definitely a reason to celebrate. It's associated with higher sales / revenue and profitability, brings in more foreign flows, and generally creates a pro-growth market atmosphere. However, very high growth, such that it brings in high inflation and consequently high interest rates, can be considered as over-heating of the economy. In economics, the very important 'ceteris paribus' ('all other things remaining unchanged') is a myth. Nothing remains constant, and intermarket connections are complex. The real skill lies in understanding which factor is likely to be more dominant than others, in a given context.

Therefore, while the GDP is a key economic metric, it's worth keeping in mind that there are several points of criticism against it that can't easily be brushed aside.

For one thing, it completely ignores unpaid labour, of the sort undertaken by housewives, say. For some developed countries, this value has been <u>calculated</u> to vary between 15% of the GDP to up to 70% of the GDP! Moreover, while the GDP measures output, it does not provide any insights into who the main beneficiaries of this output are, nor does it have anything to say about the welfare and well-being of people and the environment.

Nevertheless, for better or for worse, it's clear that the GDP is here to stay, warts and all, for at least several decades, if not much longer. So it's definitely worthwhile for investors to get a good understanding of it and various concepts associated with it. Predicting growth is the final objective of all economic analysis. Understanding growth is a must for any market analysis.

Chapter 3

Industrial Performance: Important Pillar Of The Economy

*T*he *year: around 9000 BC. The place: Jericho, in modern-day Palestine.*

This was the third year in a row that Zirtana and the rest of her band had been able to take things relatively easy. Their elders had explicitly told them to not hunt and forage for more than four hours in a day: just five years prior, most able-bodied men and women in their small settlement had to spend at least eight hours every day in the quest for food.

But it wasn't as though the elders now wanted youngsters to lounge about: in addition to hunting game, Zirtana and her fellows were also expected to help those who had made this radical societal change possible. Ever since she'd been a little girl, Zirtana had heard of a group of people who were trying to make wild barley edible — mostly in the context of jokes made at their expense. But they'd plodded on, carried on with their tinkering, and had actually succeeded in their foolhardy endeavour!

Zirtana didn't particularly enjoy working in the fields, but it sure beat being on the receiving end of a wild animal's fury.

The agricultural revolution enabled vast swathes of humanity to give up their old hunter-gatherer lifestyle, and to transition to a sedentary mode of life in permanent settlements. It also freed people up from the burden of constantly looking for food, and thus enabled people to turn their attention to specific skills, leading to the emergence of occupations requiring specialisation, such as pottery, metallurgy, masonry, woodworking, etc.

Ultimately, the agricultural revolution upended what humanity had been doing for nearly 200,000 years, and resulted in many of the cultural, social, and physical constructs we now take for granted.

But then, comparatively speaking, humanity just coasted for something like the next eleven millenia. Civilisations rose and fell, but there were no upheavals that could match the scale and impact of the agricultural revolution.

Not until the 18th century.

For that's when a series of technological advancements in Europe, now collectively considered to be part of the so-called First Industrial Revolution, changed the face of the world. The mechanisation of textile-making, more efficient steam engines, sophisticated machining tools, and improved iron production techniques were only some of the giant leaps humanity had made by the 1830s.

Since then, we've been through the Second Industrial Revolution (roughly 1870-1914; it was characterised by growing electrification and the use of the telegraph, petroleum, railroads, and steel) and the Third Industrial Revolution (in the second half of the 20th century; broadly characterised by the transition from mechanical and analogue technologies to digital ones, including transistors, microprocessors, and the Internet). In addition, it's believed that we're currently going through a Fourth Industrial Revolution characterised by interconnectivity, automation, and a blurring of the demarcations between the physical, digital, and biological spheres.

Today, the economic and social destinies of countries are inextricably bound to their degree of industrialisation and the state of their industries. Economists have discovered and developed several metrics that can help governments quantify the state of their countries' economies and ensure that they remain oriented in the right direction. In this chapter, we'll focus on three such indicators.

PMI: The Economic Oracle

Let's talk about an indicator that is rarely taught about in classroom economics, but is quite popular in the real world. The Purchasing Managers' Index (PMI) is a much-followed index globally because of the fantastic "schedule" it follows. While many (if not most) other indicators are published with a lag, the PMI comes out in the first few days of each month, and thus effectively acts as a leading indicator. The PMI is mainly calculated for two sectors, Manufacturing and Services, based on data collected by IHS Markit (now a part of S&P Global). The PMI data clearly identifies turning points in the business cycle and closely track the rate of change in key economic variables such as gross domestic product (GDP).

Historically, the PMI has had a high degree of correlation with the business cycle, and has successfully acted as a strong leading indicator. This proven track record is one of the many reasons why the PMI is so closely monitored. Owing to its timely availability and the fact that it's captured for several key economies (making cross-country comparison a possibility), it's a strong contender for being my favourite indicator.

Let's understand this indicator better by looking at the methodology used by the data collection agency, IHS Markit(now a part of S&P Global). As per its reports, the PMI was conceptualised to fulfil the following key criteria:

1. **It is based on a standard questionnaire presented to key decision makers.**

   Companies are asked a set of questions regarding output, demand, prices, and employment. The standardised questionnaire makes it possible to obtain a grassroot perspective and timely information which has a significant time advantage over the official data.

2. **Responses involve simply indicating whether the levels of a given variable are higher, lower, or unchanged compared to its levels in the previous month.**

   This makes it possible to obtain rapid and accurate responses. Since the responses can't be open-ended, there's no room for vague opinions.

3. **Data is collected from organised working groups, who are recruited and managed in such a way as to ensure an accurate representation of the underlying economic structure.**

   To increase accuracy and ease of representation, the resulting indices are also weighted. Clearly, the PMI methodology focuses on simplification and provides early signals regarding the business cycle minus the noise.

4. **The underlying survey responses included in the indices are not revised after first being published.**

The phenomenon of data revision in official data leads to ambiguity and uncertainty. There's no element of data revision when it comes to the PMI.

The complete methodology for the PMI is excellently summed up in the following flowchart:

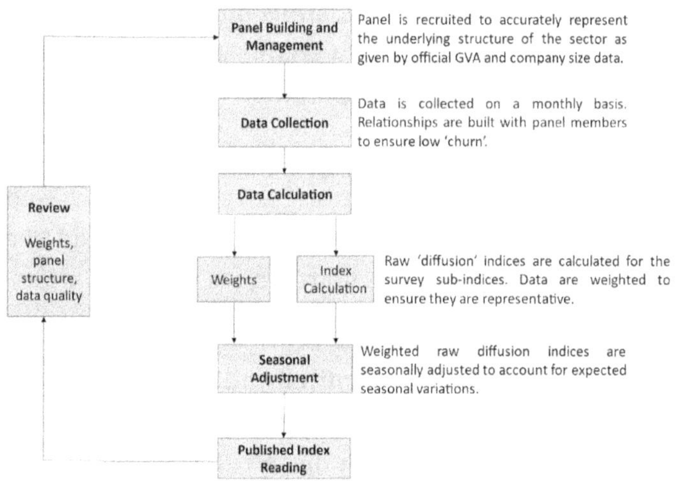

Source: IHS Markit (now S&P Global)

Questions are of the following form (using output as an example): "Is the level of output at your unit (in volume terms) higher, the same, or lower than one month ago?" Companies are also asked to provide reasons (open-ended) for the response given. All this data is usually collected during the middle two weeks of the month, so companies are asked to compare the middle of one month to that of another. All responses are input into IHS Markit's Polling Engine database for data calculation and weighting purposes.

The variables that are taken into consideration when creating the PMI readings for manufacturing and services are indicated below.

Manufacturing	Services	Composite (manufacturing and services)
Output	Business Activity	Output
New Orders	New Business	New Orders
Employment	Employment	Employment
Input Prices	Input Costs	Input prices
Output Prices	Output Prices	Output Prices
Backlogs of Work	Outstanding Business	Backlogs of Work
Future Activity	Future Activity	Future Activity
Suppliers' Delivery Times		
Quantity of Purchases		
Stocks of Purchases		
Stocks of Finished Goods		
New Export Orders		
Purchasing Managers' Index*		

Source: IHS Markit (now S&P Global)

The rows in the table above show the comparable index types for each sector and which indices for manufacturing and services are weighted together to calculate the composite readings. For example, the Manufacturing Output Index is the direct equivalent of the Services Business Activity Index and these two indices are weighted together to calculate the Composite Output Index.

An important clarification: the headline Composite Output Index is a weighted average of the headline Services Business Activity Index and the Manufacturing Output Index. The headline Manufacturing PMI is NOT used in the calculation of the Composite Output Index.

The data collected is weighted and seasonally adjusted to produce the headline indices that get published. The diffusion index (i.e. an index that indicates which industrial performance indicators are moving higher or lower, or are remaining the same) is created in such a way that a reading above 50 indicates expansion, while a reading below 50 indicates contraction. A reading of 50 indicates no change.

INDEX VALUE = (% reporting 'up') + (0.5 * (% reporting 'the same')) + (0.0 * (% reporting 'down'))

The resulting index values are therefore bounded between 0 (all companies respond 'down') and 100 (all companies respond 'up'), with a theoretical no-change mark at 50 (all companies respond 'the same' or equal proportions respond 'up' and 'down').

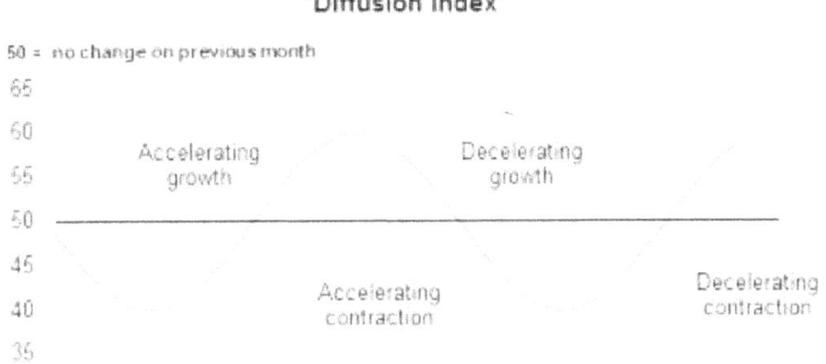

For example, take a movement in a PMI from 55.0 in January to 52.5 in February. Although the level of this index has fallen, it has nonetheless posted a level of above 50.0 in both months. The correct interpretation of this is that the volume of output expanded in both January and February, but that the rate of increase was slower in February compared to January.

Now that we understand the methodology behind the PMI in some detail, let's look at its use cases. First of all, it's a good signal of economic activity. A country's PMI moves more or less in tandem with its GDP growth rate. Similarly, the global PMI moves in sync with the global growth rate as well as global trade growth. As we know, ~60% of global growth comes from global trade and therefore global GDP and trade are related and PMI release can lead both. Secondly, the PMI can help us evaluate cross-country opportunities. When the narrative in 2022 was that India is decoupling from the rest of the world (specifically the West), the PMI offered the most concrete proof for this claim. PMI data can single-handedly help us compare different economies, given the uniformity in data collection methodology across countries.

However, the PMI's use cases are not limited to macro-economy alone. A higher PMI points to higher business activity, and therefore to higher commodities demand. A chart of China's PMI (China's the biggest consumer of commodities) or global PMI moves in lockstep with copper/commodity prices. Therefore, studying the PMI is an effective way of understanding the movement of commodity prices.

As far as the equity markets are concerned, they have a similar link to the PMI as growth. A higher PMI reading signals higher growth and consequently higher demand. Ceteris paribus (which, of course, is something economists can only ever dream of), it should straightforwardly lead to higher equity prices, but in practice, there are a large number of variables at play, some of which we have discussed in detail in the chapter on growth. However, considering the PMI to be a proxy for demand would not be completely misplaced.

Where bonds are concerned, due to a higher PMI signalling higher growth, there have been clear instances of strong PMI data leading to increased bond yields. Again, as we have reiterated throughout this book, what often ends up moving markets is unexpected aspects of macro data. If a slowdown is expected but the PMI data shows a massive expansion, bond yields will tend to jump and long-duration bonds lose money. On its own, high growth is bond-negative and equity-positive.

When it comes to currency, a relatively higher PMI should theoretically lead to the appreciation of the currency of the country in question. However, the outcome also depends heavily on inflation, central bank policies, fiscal stability, ratings, and more. It also depends on the relative PMIs of the currency pair in question.

To sum up, the PMI is an excellent indicator for quickly understanding the change in a business cycle, but it's not sufficient on its own. It needs to be married with other data points to create a holistic picture. However, we still consider it to be our favourite indicator due to its rare ability to shine a light on early signs and warnings.

Eight Core Data And The IIP

Measuring the industrial performance of the economy is critical for the markets. In India, industry contributes about 30% to the overall output. Apart from the PMI, which is a leading indicator, two other popular indicators are the Index of Industrial Production (IIP) and data from eight core industries (often simply referred to as 'eight core data'). Both these kinds of data come with a certain amount of lag. To determine concrete signals, one needs to look at the PMI, IIP, and eight core data together.

The data relating to the Index of Industrial Production (IIP) for a given month is released two months later, on the 12th. For instance, the IIP release on the 12th of May will reflect the data for the month of March. Moreover, the IIP is an index, which means that there is a base year for which its value has been set at 100. Currently, the base year is FY12.

The methodology for putting together the IIP involves finding the right sectors and weighting them in an appropriate manner. The weights of particular items (where each item is an industrial activity, such as ready-made garment manufacturing or coal mining) are generally computed in proportion to the contribution they make to the gross value added (GVA) of the broader economic activity of which they're a part, such as manufacturing, mining, construction, etc.

Individual items are included in the index basket (i.e. the set of items that construct the index) only if they provide some minimum contribution to the national product. The basket is so selected that the contribution to the national product of all the items in the basket is, say, about 80 percent. The overriding criterion for the selection of basket items is that there should be production data regularly available for them from the various data source agencies.

This is what the currently available data measures:

By Usage	Weights
IIP	100
Mining & quarrying	14
Manufacturing	78
Electricity	8

By economic activity	Weights*
IIP	100
Primary goods	34
Capital goods	8
Intermediate goods	17
Infrastructure/construction goods	12
Consumer goods	28
Consumer durables	13
Consumer non-durables	15

Rounded down to the nearest whole number

Source: MOSPI

Almost all of these categories have multiple sub-categories. For instance, manufacturing has about 23 sub-categories, and data is available individually for food products, textiles, pharmaceuticals, etc. More details on the nuances of IIP methodology can be found at https://mospi.gov.in/sites/default/files/publication_reports/manual_iip_23oct08_0.pdf

While the IIP is potentially a very useful indicator, there are two major problems associated with it:

1. **Sampling bias:** Since the IIP relies on self-reporting by industrial units, the underlying data

can get messed up if individual responding units do not respond or respond incorrectly. As a result, it's considered prudent to take a 3-month moving average of the IIP data so as to prevent sampling errors from creeping into your analyses.

2. **Availability of data:** The IIP data is only available with a lag of 1.5 months, and doesn't have much predictive value as a result: it's not a leading indicator.

While the IIP data is available in the form of an index, which is then used to calculate the headline year-on-year (YoY) changes, the eight core data used to be available in terms of exact volumes until May 2021; since then, instead of the actual volumes, only index data is being reported. The eight core data truly represents the most important industries for India's industrial output. These industries act as an accurate leading indicator for India's industrial production and manufacturing activity. The industry groups and the weights they're assigned in the current data are as follows:

Component	Units	Weight
Coal	million tonnes	10.3
Crude oil	thousand tonnes	9.0
Natural gas	million cubic metres	6.9
Refinery products	thousand tonnes	28.0
Fertilisers	thousand tonnes	2.6
Steel	thousand tonnes	17.9
Cement	thousand tonnes	5.4
Electricity	million Kwh	19.9

Source: Ministry of Commerce & Industry

These eight core industries represent 40% of the total industrial production (IP). For the purpose of interpretation, looking at coal, electricity, natural gas, and refinery products together offers a comprehensive outlook on energy production in India. Fertiliser production can be used to interpret the rural economy and the domestic supply of fertilisers; in addition, to some extent, it provides a top-level view of fertiliser companies in India. Steel and cement are integral components of infrastructure and construction activity in India. These eight core industries form the backbone of the Indian economy as we know it.

However, economies are changing fast. Data and digital innovation can contribute immensely to output in the coming years. This is not captured in the traditional way of boiling output down to eight core industries. The actual pillars of economies are fast evolving.

I reiterate here that the eight core data, IIP, and manufacturing PMI should ideally move in the same direction to create robust signals of industrial performance. The importance of these indicators lies in the fact that they have some power to predict economic growth, especially the sub-components of mining, manufacturing, and construction. In other words, the movements of the IIP and the PMI are correlated with growth. However, because of the availability of sectoral data, a certain amount of extrapolation can also yield some understanding of broad sectoral trends in the economy, the urban-rural divide, the divide between labour-intensive and capital-intensive sectors, and so on.

Thus, robust industrial sector data is typically indicative of a stronger currency, higher yields, and better equity performance: the same effects as those of growth which we looked at in the earlier chapter. However, nothing remains ceteris paribus, and every macro-regime needs to be studied with a fresh pair of eyes.

Also, it should be remembered that leading indicators are the holy grail of finance/economics, and the fact that we have not one but two indicators (the PMI because it comes in early and the eight core data because it can throw light on industrial activity ahead) that come close to being leading indicators is a boon for analysts and experts.

Chapter 4

External Situation: We Are Just One Ship In Global Waters

Your alarm blares insistently, unwilling to simmer down until its purpose of waking you up is fulfilled. It finally succeeds, and gets an angry slap for its efforts.

You yawn and make your way to the kitchen for some breakfast. As you sip your filter coffee and bite into your apple, your mind wanders to the good old days when you used to have hot chocolate on Saturdays, and that special and exorbitantly priced Colombian coffee on Sundays. Not to mention the Kiwis and Tunisian dates you'd bite into whenever the fancy struck you.

Those days are gone now.

As you put on your work clothes, you spot a rather large stain on your collar. Drat! Must've spilled some food during the office party last week. You curse your clumsiness. You can't afford to be so careless with your work clothes. They cost nearly twice as much as during that wonderful bygone era when the cheaper Bangladesh-made stuff was everywhere.

Before you step out of your house, you make sure you have two grand in cash safely tucked away in your wallet: you know your car's fuel tank is nearly empty, and that cash should be enough for around four litres of petrol.

Once you've clambered into the driver's seat, you furtively look around, making sure there's nobody in the vicinity. You then slowly open your satchel and pull out a smartphone, making sure to keep it on your lap, as low as possible, away from the prying eyes of any busybodies who might report you. After all, being caught red-handed with a black market product would be cause for at least a hefty fine, if not worse.

"Leaving now, be there in 15", is the message you send to your best friend. It's your turn today to get him to his office. Not only does it save a lot of money, but it's also nice to have company when you're waiting in the serpentine queues at the petrol pumps.

"Cool, I'll be waiting", types your friend on his smartphone… also a black-market piece.

Chocolate and fancy coffee: unaffordable. Kiwi and Tunisian dates: not available. Petrol: pay through your nose for it. Smartphones and laptops: you can buy them only in the shady parts of town.

This is the kind of dystopian country we'd be living in if, for whatever reason, we were to suddenly become an isolationist country and completely cut off all trade with external countries. Our lives would be bleak and cheerless, perhaps not unlike East Germany before the Berlin Wall fell. Many technologies, products, and commodities that we take for granted would have to be smuggled into the country and then bought on the sly.

This scenario just goes to underscore the importance of foreign trade. Coffee imported from Columbia, Kiwis from New Zealand, and oil bought on the cheap from Qatar: we get to enjoy these commodities only thanks to foreign trade!

So let's take a closer look at this vital practice, understand some of the basic economics behind it, and then see how it typically affects investors.

The Basics Of Foreign Trade

The term 'foreign trade' is rather self-explanatory: it refers to the exchange of goods and services between different countries. Foreign trade plays a crucial role in the global economy and is essential for the growth and development of individual countries. It enables countries to specialise in the production of certain goods and services, and to access a wider range of products at competitive prices. Global trade contributes around approximately 60% to world GDP and is the single largest measure of globalisation.

As far as India is concerned, on the 15th of every month, the Ministry of Commerce releases detailed foreign trade numbers. As one might expect, this report is headlined by the total monthly imports, total monthly exports, and the trade balance. However, the data in the report goes much deeper than that. The data is presented using so-called 'Harmonised System' (HS) codes, and typically includes commodity-wise numbers.

The Harmonised System is a standardised numerical system used to classify and identify goods that are traded internationally. It was developed by the World Customs Organisation (WCO) to facilitate international trade by providing a uniform system for classifying goods in customs declarations. A basic HS code consists of six digits, with additional digits being used for a more detailed classification. The codes are arranged in a hierarchical manner, with broader categories at the higher levels and more specific categories at the lower levels.

The data in the Ministry of Commerce's report speaks volumes about India's economy. For instance, when textile stocks do well, there's almost always a corresponding increase in India's textile exports. This is because a rise in exports is good for sales, and hence for stock prices as well. Similarly, the amount of oil that's imported highlights the impact of higher oil prices on

India's external situation and has many repercussions on the various asset classes.

The Trade Balance

Let's start with the absolute basics. India's trade involves two broad categories: goods (cars, wines, wheat, and the list goes on) and services (such as IT and telecom consultancy). Exports are the goods / services we send out to the rest of the world, typically in exchange for dollars. Imports are the goods / services we buy from the rest of the world, and which we pay for in dollars. The difference between the monetary value of imports and exports is called the trade balance. When the value of imports is higher than that of exports, we get what's called a trade deficit (this is usually the case for India's foreign trade in goods). When the opposite is true, we get what's called a trade surplus (this is the case for India's foreign trade in services).

India is one of the world's leading exporters of services. In FY20, the value of India's net exports in services was estimated to be USD 84 billion. By FY23, this number had shot up to a whopping USD 138 billion. There are two major components to India's net service exports: Computer / Software Services (e.g. conventional IT services) and Business Services (e.g. legal, accounting, and auditing services). While software has long been the bellwether of service exports, business services have been contributing more and more to it over the past several years. India's stellar performance in service exports is now capable of reducing the dent from structural goods deficit.

The trade balance, by virtue of its effect on the country's balance of payments or BOP (i.e. a metric summarising India's economic transactions with foreign countries), has a direct impact on the currency. A trade surplus makes a case for domestic currency appreciation because in that situation, for a constant amount of domestic currency, the amount of dollars in the economy increases. Conversely, a trade deficit implies that dollars exit the economy (we pay more than we earn) and thus make a case against the domestic currency.

However, I believe that the trade balance tells us a lot more than that: in truth, it's also a measure of a country's economic and political priorities. Even after the US had imposed a ban on Chinese goods as part of famous 'Trade War', data showed that exports to the US from China and its neighbouring countries had only gone up. The conclusion? Chinese exports were being re-routed into the US through other countries. Similarly, if the volume of imports of certain goods (such as auto parts) into India were to go down, it would validate the success of policies like 'Make in India'. If the import of electronic components is going up, but at the same time, the export of finished electronic goods such as mobiles is also increasing, then it can be concluded that the economy is adding value to raw materials and then exporting the resulting products.

Again, policy decisions as to what an economy must produce domestically can be taken by looking at the goods that have the highest import level as well as high domestic consumption. For example, if an economy includes many children, its consumption of toys will be higher, so it should aim to produce more cost-effective toys domestically. Foreign policies also get reflected via trade agreements, such as the various kinds of Free Trade Agreements (FTAs) that usually exist between friendly nations. Signing of relevant FTAs can make an economy and its exports more competitive.

Around 30 percent of our imports consist of oil and petroleum products. Every time oil prices rise by USD 10 per barrel, our trade balance takes a hit of around USD 15 billion annually. Engineering goods, which include transport equipment, metal products etc., are the largest non-oil contributors to India's imports (17%). India procures large chunks of its imports from China (13%), the UAE (7%), and the USA (7%). As for our exports, agricultural goods make up 11% of them, and engineering goods make up another major chunk, followed by chemicals. 17% of India's total exports go to the USA, and 7% to the UAE.

Two Key Measures

There's more to trade than meets the eye. However, for now, we'll switch gears and take a closer look at two other important measures of the external situation of the country: the current account balance (CAB) and the balance of payments (BOP).

The CAB can be broken up into four components:

a) **Trade in goods:** the import-export of goods such as machinery, jewellery, oil, cars etc. India usually has a deficit here, that is, imports are higher than exports *(so dollars go out)*.

b) **Trade in services:** the import-export of services such as IT, business processing etc. India usually has a surplus here, that is, the dollar value of the services provided is higher than that of the services received *(so dollars come in)*.

c) **Primary income:** this represents the net inflow or outflow of the income earned by the residents of a country due to their participation in economic activity abroad, such as the wages earned by expatriate workers or the profits earned by multinational corporations. For instance, if you have a cousin who's an Indian citizen but lives and works in the USA for a project, then the primary income would include her wages. For India, this number is usually negative, that is, more income is earned by foreigners in India than by Indians abroad *(so dollars go out)*.

d) **Secondary income:** this represents the net inflow or outflow of funds transferred between residents and non-residents, such as remittances sent by foreign workers to their home countries, or foreign aid given by one country to another. So if someone living in Middle East sends money to their family in India, the fund flow will be recorded here. For India, this number is usually positive — the remittances received by resident Indians are greater in total value than the ones that get sent out *(so dollars come in)*.

When the value of incoming dollars is greater than that of outgoing dollars, the current account is in a surplus. When the inverse is true, the current account is in a deficit. Due to the nature of its economy, India's current account is almost always in a deficit. In FY21, however, we recorded a current account surplus because the trade deficit had massively shrunk due to reduced imports during the COVID-19 pandemic.

The RBI usually releases India's CAB numbers with a lag of one quarter; for instance, the data for the April-June quarter will be available towards the end of of September. An improvement in the current account is considered to have a positive effect on the domestic currency, while a worsening current account leads to currency depreciation.

Over the years, the remittances received by India have improved considerably. Moreover, before COVID-19, India used to clock net service exports worth USD 6 billion per month. Today, this number is closer to USD 12 billion per month, i.e., an additional USD 72 billion a year. Both these developments are green shoots that point towards a more sustainable current account position for India in the coming years.

Now, let's move on to the second key measure of a country's external situation: the balance of payments (BOP). In addition to the current account, the BOP has two more components:

a) **Capital account:** the capital account primarily includes capital transfers, which refer to transfers of financial assets and liabilities without being accompanied by any corresponding economic transactions. Examples of such transfers are debts that are forgiven, inherited estates, and donations. The capital account also includes transactions related to the acquisition and disposal of non-produced, non-financial assets such as patents, copyrights, and trademarks. In the Indian context, this usually works out to be a relatively small negative number.

b) **Financial account:** the financial account can be majorly divided into two subcategories: direct investment and portfolio investment. Direct investment refers to transactions that result in a lasting interest in foreign enterprises, such as the establishment of a subsidiary or the acquisition of a controlling stake in a foreign company. This category is captured under the rubric of Foreign Direct Investment (FDI). Portfolio investment, on the other hand, refers to transactions that involve the purchase or sale of financial assets such as stocks, bonds, and other securities. This category is captured under the rubric of Foreign Institutional Investor (FII) flows, which are usually closely and widely watched. Separately, External Commercial Borrowings (ECBs) are also a part of financial account. ECBs refer to funds borrowed by eligible entities from foreign sources such as international banks, financial institutions, and international capital markets. Simply put, fund flow from an Indian company raising capital abroad via financial instruments such as bonds will be classified under ECBs.

In quantitative terms,

BOP = current account (usually negative) + capital account (usually negative but small in magnitude) + financial account (usually positive)

What The BOP Indicates

Now that we understand the various line items in the BOP, let's understand what it's really used for. The BOP indicates the total inflow and outflow of dollars in the economy. If more dollars are coming in than are going out (i.e. in a state of BOP surplus), the excess dollars get added to Foreign Exchange Reserves (FX reserves). If more dollars are going out than are coming in, the deficit gets paid out of the existing FX reserves. Depending on how young you are, you might remember the infamous Indian BOP crisis of 1991. That crisis was triggered by a combination of factors, including a sharp increase in oil prices, a rise in global interest rates, and a decline in the country's export competitiveness. As a result, the current account deficit widened to nearly 3.5% of GDP (more than USD 5 billion in absolute terms), while foreign exchange reserves fell to a dangerously low level of less than USD 1 billion.

It was in response to this crisis that the Indian government implemented a series of economic reforms, and this period is now usually referred as the 'Liberalisation' of the Indian economy. This included liberalising trade and investment policies, devaluing the national currency, and dismantling the complex system of industrial licensing and permits. These reforms helped restore confidence in the economy and attracted foreign investment, leading to a significant improvement in India's BOP position. Today, the Reserve Bank of India maintains a healthy USD 500 billion + quantum in its forex reserves.

'Import cover' is a term used to measure a country's ability to pay for its imports using its foreign exchange reserves. It is calculated as the ratio of a country's total foreign exchange reserves to its total monthly imports. For instance, if India has USD 550 billion in forex reserves, and imports are roughly USD 55 billion a month, the import cover will be of 10 months.

This is considered an important indicator for understanding the external position of countries. It should be remembered that history is marred with crises arising due to a lack of foreign exchange reserves, be it the 1997 Asian Financial Crisis (triggered due to Thailand running low on forex reserves) or the ongoing (as of 2023) Sri Lankan Crisis (triggered due to Sri Lanka's inability to repay its foreign debt obligations as a result of insufficient forex reserves). Thus, having healthy levels of forex reserves is critical for proper economic functioning.

The lion's share of India's debt doesn't come from external economies. However, the countries that do borrow abroad need to have healthy forex reserves along with a good growth rate in order to be able to service the debt at the appropriate time.

Let's now understand the role of external situation indicators on different asset classes and investments.

Foreign Trade And The Markets

The asset class that is most directly affected by a country's external situation is currency. All economic activity that brings in dollars on a net basis, result in domestic currency appreciation. Improvements in the trade balance, CAB, or overall BOP, as well as improvements in any sub-parts of theirs, such as the FDI or FII, all strengthen the domestic currency.

However, part of the RBI's mandate is to prevent wild currency fluctuations. As a result, the RBI can choose to intervene in the currency markets, and does in fact regularly do so. When the INR is depreciating due to weak fundamentals (high trade deficit, high current account deficit, FII outflows, etc.), the RBI can reduce its forex reserves and soothe the market with dollars that are not otherwise coming in. This helps put a damper on depreciation. Similarly, when dollar inflows are strong, the RBI can use the incoming dollars to add to its forex reserves, thus slowing down currency appreciation. RBI tends to avoid currency volatility in either direction. A stable currency serves as a solid foundation for economic growth.

Commodities aren't severely affected directly by a country's external situation, but their pricing can change due to currency movements. For instance, if the external situation is worsening, domestic currency depreciation can lead to higher INR returns on gold, even if the global price of gold is stable.

Debt markets do keep a close eye on the external situation. A weaker external position can lead to currency depreciation, which in turn increases inflation (the cost of imported goods go up) and discourages central banks from going easy on monetary policy. This has a negative impact on the bond markets. In such a situation, higher interest rates can fend off currency depreciation to some extent, but may not be great for debt markets, depending on other macro fundamentals. On the flip side, a depreciating currency makes domestic bonds attractive for foreign investors and the additional flows can help demand side of bonds, thus possibly reducing yields or increasing prices. A high BOP deficit can warrant raising more money in the form of debt in order to service the deficit, which can negatively affect yields. In general, a worsening external situation leads to higher yields, but it depends crucially on other macro variables (remember: 'ceteris paribus' is a lie!)

Equity markets also keep a close eye on the external situation. Most importantly, a strong external position leads to a positive investor sentiment, which leads to better equity performance. However, it's also true that a depreciating currency can boost the performance of export-oriented sectors and can make domestic markets lucrative to foreigners.

Looked at through an equity-oriented lens, every little detail of the external situation matters. Which sectors are exporting more? Which new trade agreements have been signed? Which sectors are successfully seeing import substitution? What is the cost advantage that other countries have? Which raw materials are getting imported at a lower cost than before? What will be the impact on rates? The list goes on. The moral is: Indian investors must do their best to understand India's external position in order to make sound judgements from an equity perspective.

Foreign trade is an inevitable component of any economy, and probably has been ever since nation-states have existed. After all, no country can be a self-sufficient island: even North Korea, where self-reliance is a core principle baked into its state ideology *Juche*, is heavily reliant on its trading ties with China!

Moreover, changes in the kinds of goods and services that a country imports and exports can also serve as a barometer of the economic developments within a country. As a result, tracking trends in foreign trade data can yield valuable insights to investors who go the extra mile.

Chapter 5

Fiscal Policy: Union Budget And More

It's a well-known saying that there are only two certainties in life: death and taxes.

And while the thought of paying taxes is one we all dread, taxation is ultimately vital for all of us, as it's effectively a form of capital raising by governments that lets them execute plans that matter.

And the policy that a government lays out in order to specify how much money it will raise through taxes and other means, and where and how all this money will be spent, so as to influence the economy, is called the fiscal policy.

An interesting aside: it's likely that good fiscal policies had a role to play in ensuring that we don't live in a Nazi-dominated world today!

What's the connection, you ask? Well, you see, after the Great Depression struck the US in 1929, Americans lost their jobs in droves, and didn't have access to basic necessities like food and shelter. As the country struggled to recover, President Franklin D. Roosevelt implemented a series of fiscal policies that would come to be known as the New Deal.

Roosevelt and his advisers believed that government spending could help jumpstart the economy and create jobs. They also believed that taxes could be used to redistribute wealth and reduce income inequality.

Among many other things, Roosevelt created the Federal Emergency Relief Administration (FERA), which provided direct financial assistance to unemployed Americans. He also introduced the Social Security Act, which established a system of old-age pensions and disability insurance.

At the same time, Roosevelt used the tax code to promote economic growth and reduce inequality. He introduced progressive income taxes, which levied higher rates on those with higher incomes. He also raised taxes on corporations and implemented a number of new taxes, such as the estate tax and the gift tax.

This bold and innovative response worked: Roosevelt and his advisors were indeed able to create jobs, stimulate economic growth, and provide relief to those in need. This not only healed America's economy, but also ensured Roosevelt's re-election.

As a result, by the time Pearl Harbour was bombed, the US was economically capable of engaging in a war, and the decisive Roosevelt was able to lead his country through most of the rest of World War 2. Who knows what would have happened if this had not been the case?!

Now that we've underscored the potentially world-changing importance of good fiscal policies, let's take a deep dive into the fiscal policies of India in particular.

The Union Budget

Probably the biggest annual economic event in India is the budget announcement, and this event also serves to publicly lay out the government's planned fiscal policy. However, although this event hogs most of the attention given to fiscal policy by market-watchers, the truth is that fiscal policy affects the markets every single day. After all, government bond yields depend on government borrowings, which is a measure of the supply of government bonds. On the flip side, the market's appetite for government borrowings is indicative of the demand side. And the bond yields alone can affect and condition the performance of other asset classes.

If all of this is getting too much for you, let's take a step back and start by simply focusing on understanding the Union Budget — the fiscal policy's first point of contact with the world at large.

The Union Budget of India is announced on 1 February every year. In the weeks prior to this date, the mainstream media spends a fair amount of time covering the various expectations experts and analysts have from the budget; similarly, in the weeks following this date, the media unpacks the budget's multitude of implications. Being able to understand and analyse the budget is an incredibly useful ability for all investors, so let's try to add this ability to our arsenal.

Like all budgets, government budgets also have two parts: the revenue side and the expenditure side. The revenue side represents the government's various sources of money. These can be classified as being either tax revenue, non-tax revenue, or non-debt capital receipts. Let's understand each of these in detail.

Tax Revenue

Tax revenue, as the name suggests, is the revenue that the government earns through taxes. There are two main kinds of taxes: direct taxes and indirect taxes. Direct taxes are taxes that are levied on the earnings of an individual or organisation. For instance, income tax and corporate tax are kinds of direct taxes. Income tax, as we all know, is a tax paid on the earnings of an individual. Corporate tax is the tax paid on the profits made by an organisation.

So far, so good.

Now, once the Union Budget is out, the tricky part is figuring out whether the numbers are credible. A transparent, credible set of budget numbers is the gold standard for economic certainty and confidence. As a rule of thumb, corporate tax and income tax each contribute close to 3% of GDP, +/- 50 bps. From the budget's perspective, the number that needs to be the most credible one is the nominal GDP growth figure; most of the other important numbers can be derived from the overall output numbers.

Hypothetically, if the nominal GDP goes up from 100 units to 110 units (i.e. a 10% growth), then the corporate and income tax revenues will be close to 3.3 units each. When there are changes in the tax regime, however, these numbers can vary a fair bit more. For instance, when India cut the corporate tax rate in FY20 to a flat 25%, the corporate-tax-to-GDP ratio fell to 2.7%.

Similarly, when income tax cuts and tweaks are announced, an appropriate fiscal burden is also announced in order to take their tax revenue impact for the Government into consideration. Direct taxes contribute a bit more than half of the overall gross tax revenue.

Indirect Taxes

The rest comes from a range of indirect taxes — taxes that are paid on goods and services. The most important such taxes are customs duty, excise duty, and the Goods and Services Tax (GST). Unlike direct taxes, whose collection rates grow at a relatively steady pace, these taxes can change in a more unpredictable manner. For instance, when global oil prices rise significantly, the government may need to slash the excise duty rate to keep domestic oil prices in check. Something just like this happened in early 2022: in the wake of global crude prices shooting up amidst the Russia-Ukraine war, the Indian government reduced the excise duty in order to put a ceiling on the pump prices that end consumers had to pay. On the flip side, during good times or when global crude prices are falling, the government can keep pump prices constant and earn more revenue through taxes.

The estimates for excise duty revenue should be rational, should indicate the government's expectations for crude prices in the coming year, and should also represent the final pump price acceptable to it.

Another common kind of indirect tax is customs duty; the projected revenue through this duty serves as an indicator of the amount and types of imports expected. Usually, the customs duty tends to grow at a rate that's rather close to the nominal GDP growth rate.

Lastly, there's the closely tracked Goods and Services Tax, which is more than just an indicator of the government's finances. The projected revenue from GST is indicative of the buoyancy in the economy, and the ongoing growth and consumption in the economy. In addition, in theory, GST rates should keep pace with growth rates; however, since the GST tax regime is a relatively new one, the tax base associated with it grew much faster in its initial years when a large number of users were first adopting it. This base should stabilise in the near future.

GST revenue is shared between the Centre and states in an almost 1:1 ratio for most goods and services. For instance, if a good is sold at 18% GST, 9% goes to the Centre and 9% goes to the states. The revenue amount indicated in the Union Budget only reflects the Centre's share.

The sum of all the taxes discussed above equals the Gross Tax Revenue, which totals roughly 11% of the nominal GDP.

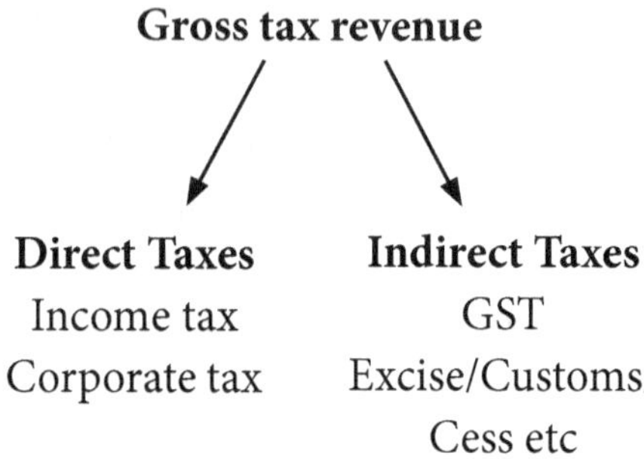

From the taxes received by the Centre, ~30% goes to the states, union territories, and the National Calamity Contingent Duty (NCCD). Between the 11th Finance Commission and the 14th, the share of net proceeds recommended to be devolved to the states increased from 29.5% to 42%. Net proceeds are defined in Article 279 of the Constitution as the Centre's Gross Tax Revenue less surcharges, cesses, and the cost of collection.

A question I'm often asked is: if the recorded GST revenue is already only the Centre's share, then why is an additional deduction applicable to it? The short answer is that as per the Finance Commission, the deduction is on the entire Gross Tax Revenue accrued to the government and does not concern GST alone. Therefore, all tax payments accrued to centre (along with centre's share of GST) is taken into account to calculate the transfer to states. When the amount that will devolve to the states is considered, what we're finally left with is the **net tax revenue.**

Net Tax Revenue= Gross Tax Revenue- Transfer to States

Non-Tax Sources Of Revenue

Tax revenue is augmented by two more sources: non-tax revenue and non-debt capital receipts. Non-tax revenue is revenue received in the form of interest and dividends from banks (including the RBI), various public sector undertakings, etc. Typically, the RBI dividend (which was rationalised by the 'Jalan committee') draws a lot of attention. One reason for this is that this component is directly related to central banks' profitability and can grow disproportionately in good years. Non-tax revenue does well when PSUs do well as there is larger transfer that gets accrued to the Government's kitty.

The final component is non-debt capital receipts, the major chunk of which consists of disinvestments. A disinvestment involves the government liquidating its assets in a public sector enterprise partially or fully. This results in revenue generation for the government, but also encourages the creation of more efficient enterprises. For instance, sale of Air India is a classic case of divestments. India's real fling with divestment started in the last decade when in FY15, we clocked a healthy INR 320 billion and improved this number to INR 420 billion in FY16. FY17 was a bit lacklustre but in FY18, we clocked the highest ever INR 1 trillion in divestment proceeds, a very healthy 0.6% of GDP. This was much higher than the budgeted INR 725 billion. In FY19, we budgeted INR 800 billion and went on to achieve INR 945 billion. Two years of consecutively overshooting budgeted estimates by a handsome margin led us to probably overestimate the divestment budget in subsequent years. In FY20, FY21 and FY22, we achieved 48%, 18% and 45% of the target, respectively. CPSE (Central Public Sector Enterprise) to CPSE sales, flow money in PSU ETFs, Further Public Offering (FPOs), Initial Public Offering(IPOs) of government owned entities are some of the possible vehicles of divestments.

Thus:
Net tax revenue (Gross Tax Revenue - states' share)
+ Non-tax revenue
+ Non-debt capital receipts (mainly disinvestments)
= Total revenue of the government

Expenditure

On the expenditure side, the two main components are revenue expenditure and capital expenditure. Revenue expenditure is best understood as the government's operating expenditure, plus the amounts it spends on certain schemes. For instance, wages, pensions, and the sums spent on MGNREGA, PM-KISAN, etc. all fall under revenue expenditure. An important point to be noted in this regard is that revenue expenditure does not create any tangible assets.

Capital expenditure, on the other hand, leads to the creation of tangible assets such as roads, railways, infrastructure etc. Revenue expenditure is recurring in nature, while capital expenditure mostly consists of one-time expenses. Revenue expenditure feeds the workforce through wages and pensions. Capital expenditure, on the other hand, creates fresh jobs. When a new road is due to be constructed, many workers need to be employed.

A budget with a higher-than-usual revenue expenditure is typically said to be a "populist" budget, whereas a budget with a focus on capital expenditure is typically considered to be focused on the economy's long-term prospects.

An increase in government expenditure creates demand (by increasing the money supply), and is therefore considered inflationary. However, we should also note that increasing the capital expenditure is relatively less inflationary because it affects both demand and supply at the level of the economy. It not only creates demand as there's more money, it also leads to the creation of new goods and services. In contrast, revenue expenditure creates no new goods and only possibly increases demand by increasing the money supply; for this reason, it is considered relatively more inflationary.

It would be unfair to end this section without mentioning the IEBR (internal and extra budgetary resources), which have become a key highlight of India's budgets. These off-balance-sheet resources are borrowed by the government via a PSU. For instance, if the food subsidy is X, half of X could come directly from the centre's pocket (technically known as Gross Budgetary

Support (GBS)) and the remaining half could come via the Food Corporation of India (FCI — the relevant PSU in this case) adding some debt to its balance sheet. This raises the overall level of public borrowing in the system.

Thus, on the plus side, we can imagine the IEBR as augmenting the capex announced in the budget to yield the true total capex of the economy. On the negative side, however, the higher level of public borrowing raises concerns of resources being crowded out by the public sector.

Fiscal Deficit

At this point, let's move on to the closely tracked fiscal deficit, which is defined as the difference between the total revenue and expenditure of the government. This number is usually studied as a percentage of the nominal GDP for a given year and is almost always the biggest news headline. As per the Fiscal Responsibility and Budget Management (FRBM) act, India is supposed to maintain a fiscal deficit target of 3% of GDP. However, during times of crisis, such as the COVID-19 pandemic, this target was abandoned to protect the growth of the economy.

The government running a deficit essentially means that its expenditure is higher than its revenue. How does its expenditure get financed, in that case? Well, there are many other sources of available to government to finance its excess expenditure. These sources and the amounts they represented in the recent past are summarised below:

	FY23RE*	FY24BE*
Gross fiscal deficit (in trillions of INR)	17.6	17.9
Sources: (as% of the gross fiscal deficit)		
Net market borrowings	63	62
Gross market borrowings	87	92
(-) Repayments	24	30
Short-term borrowings	6	3
Net external assistance	1	1
Receipts from small savings, PPF, and deposit scheme	25	26
Receipts from state provident fund	1	1
Other capital receipts	5	3
Cash balance decrease (+) / increase (-)	0	-1

Source: Budget Documents

**RE indicates revised estimates and BE indicates budget estimates. As a matter of fact, every budget announces 3 types of numbers: actual and audited numbers for the year gone by, revised estimates (RE) for the ongoing fiscal year, and budget estimates (BE) for the next fiscal year. For instance, the budget announced on 1 Feb 2023 released actual numbers for FY22, revised numbers for FY23, and budgeted numbers for FY24. The actual numbers don't usually change, the revised numbers adjust the current year's estimates based on the macro environment that has prevailed during Apr-Jan, and the budget estimates are just rational expectations for the future. The above table says that ~62% of fiscal deficit is expected to be financed by market borrowings and another ~26% is estimated to be financed through small savings, PPF etc.*

Let's understand some of these sources. The 'gross market borrowings' is the total value of the securities that will be issued in order to raise funds from the markets. Adjusted for repayments during the year under consideration, we get the 'net market borrowings', which finances roughly 60% of government expenditure in the near term.

When it comes to market securities, who are the key demand creators for them? Well, the split looks something like this:

	Ownership Pattern of Central Govt Dated Securities (% share in outstanding)
Commercial Banks	38
Insurance Companies	26.3
RBI	16.1
Provident Funds	4.8
Mutual Funds	2.3
Co-operative Banks	1.8
State Governments	1.8
Corporates	1.5
FPIs	1.4
Financial Institutions	1.1
Others	5

Source: RBI, data for FY22

Most securities are held by commercial banks and insurance companies, with most other participants being relatively small. With the RBI acting as a supporter for government financing and security purchases, its share has gone up a fair bit in the past years.

Let's continue looking at other available resources to the government to fund its deficit. Short-term borrowings consist of treasury bills etc. External assistance can include any aid received, such as from multilateral organisations. Receipts from small savings etc. mainly consist of the sums deposited (mainly by the retail masses) in government schemes such as the Kisan Vikas Patra. All of these together help finance the central government's deficit.

Next, let's take a closer look at the effects of government borrowings on various asset classes.

The Impact Of Government Debt On Assets

For starters, India's fiscal deficit doesn't affect commodities directly since commodity prices are set via global demand and supply. When the US fiscal deficit is high, the money supply in the US is also high, which can weaken its currency (the USD). When the dollar weakens, gold and commodities starts to benefit, often enormously. There could be other second level linkages; for instance, the fiscal support of the government in China could spur a demand for base metals and could therefore increase metal prices. India's fiscal deficit has no major direct bearing on commodities.

As far as currency is concerned, theoretically, a higher fiscal deficit should lead to currency depreciation. This is because money supply tends to go up. Things can be different in reality, however. If the increase in government expenditure is supporting growth without creating inflation, it can even have a positive impact on the relevant currency. It also depends on what the other countries are doing and what kind of macro-regime are we sitting in.

However, if the increase in the fiscal deficit is conditioned by the inflationary (revenue) expenditure, then yes, the currency could depreciate. Even then, it would matter what other economies were doing — we live in an interconnected world after all! If all economies are incurring high expenses, effects have to be calculated accordingly. In general, foreign institutional investors (FIIs) and rating agencies are kinder to economies that are still growing, even if with some manageable government support.

For equity, the thumb rule is that growth-supporting fiscal expenditure is good. If it comes in the form of dole-outs in specific sectors that could increase the consumption in those sectors, then the latter will benefit (for instance, think about subsidies on Electric Vehicles)!

Unless the fiscal policy is so inflationary that it leads to the monetary policy raising interest rates, equity markets usually cheer fiscal expenditure.

Now let's address the elephant in the room: the debt markets. Ideally, the bond markets will want the government to issue as few securities as possible for borrowing, in which case the supply will be lower, the demand will be adequate, and the yields will head lower to make capital gains for the bond.

Lower borrowing also implies lower expenditure and hence lower inflation, and therefore a lower probability of the central bank increasing interest rates. In a nutshell, bond markets want as low a fiscal deficit as possible. In real life, bond markets depend heavily on the 'expectations vs. surprise' element. Is the deficit higher/lower than expected? Is the deficit getting financed by markets at a higher/lower price? Which tenor (duration) is most of the borrowing occurring with? Is the RBI stepping in to create additional demand? All these are relevant questions to consider when understanding bond markets from a fiscal policy angle.

Fiscal policy has a huge impact on us all, and staying abreast of it is a good idea for investors. Currently, it's not the case that most policy measures are announced during the union budget. Instead, most of them are announced during the course of the year. For instance, additional subsidies, the change to debt fund taxation, and even the watershed cut in corporate tax were all announced on a non-budget day. Budget maths is important, but tracking it over the year is even more important. Easy fiscal policy supports growth but brings with it the possibility of higher inflation and higher interest rates.

'Fiscal prudence' is very well-rewarded in current times. It's all about when to go pro-cyclical and when to go counter-cyclical. For instance, during the Covid-19 pandemic, when growth was dwindling, the government increased its expenditure to support growth: an example of a counter-cyclical policy. However, we were still more prudent than the West. Fiscal policy is also about deciding when to focus on the short term and when to focus on a longer-term vision. There are costs and benefits to every policy decision.

Monetary Policy: Well-Tracked And Overly Critiqued

All the way back in 33 CE, the citizens of the Roman empire were witness to an unexpected financial crisis.

At that time, there was an old law on the books that required moneylenders to own a certain amount of farmland in Italy. Nobody really took it very seriously, though, and it wasn't really enforced. However, various events had begun causing the price of real estate and farmland to drop, which was not something the government was very happy about.

So how did it decide to intervene? Well, it started enforcing the old law mentioned above, which meant that lenders who'd ignored that law until then were forced to quickly buy Italian farmland. In order to do so, they asked many of their debtors to pay up early, leaving many members of the citizenry scrambling for cash. To get that cash, many people started selling their properties at lower-than-market prices, thus further reducing the price of real estate and farmland: exactly the opposite effect of what the government had intended!

In addition, several banks began failing due to bank runs, and loans became more difficult and expensive to obtain. Ultimately, the government had to step in: it formed a commission of senators who had the wherewithal to provide interest-free loans to landowners. In addition, large amounts of agricultural land were used to secure these loans. It worked, and the crisis abated! And unbeknownst to the Romans of the time, some key aspects of the way this problem was solved would see a major resurgence two thousand years later.

It makes sense for a government to address major economic problems through whatever means it can: even in an autocracy or monarchy, economic stability is bound to be a good thing for the ruler as well.

Over time, disorganised groups of lenders gave way to the first modern banks in the middle ages, and such banks eventually began to be tasked by governments to help them ensure economic stability: one of the main functions of what are now called 'central banks'.

Most central banks around the world were established during the last two centuries. Along with the maintenance of economic stability, several other functions came within their ambit, including managing forex and gold reserves, supervising other banks, minting coins and notes, and determining the monetary policy (which involves using the official interest rate and various other techniques to control the money supply and consequent growth and inflation in an economy).

Most developed countries realised rather quickly that letting elected officials tinker with a central bank's policies would be a bad idea, since politicians are prone to short-term thinking due to the election cycle. As a result, most major countries grant their central banks a large degree of autonomy, meaning that they're not beholden to the government, and can decide their policies and courses of action free from outside interference.

However, in a seemingly desperate but much needed attempt to deal with the 2008 financial crisis, the US's central bank, the Federal Reserve, began applying an action that had been tried out in Japan previously: it started buying government bonds in order to provide the US government with the funding that it could then try and use to stimulate economic activity.

This interventionary technique, called Quantitative Easing (QE), bears some resemblance to the solution to the Roman crisis we saw above, in that it too involves introducing a large amount of liquidity into the economy. While QE remains somewhat controversial, the Federal Reserve seems to have adopted it rather wholeheartedly to abate financial crises. And why not? Today's central banks are largely autonomous but continue to function as lenders of last resort to the government.

Another potentially promising approach to tough financial situations goes by the name 'Modern Monetary Theory (MMT)'. What the MMT basically holds is that as long as the economy is printing its own currency, it can go beyond its foreseeable revenue streams to spend. Simply put, governments implementing the MMT do not rely on taxes or borrowing for spending, since they can print as much as they need and are the monopoly issuers of the currency. While the term was coined by Bill Mitchell, an Australian economist in the 90s, it only really came into the limelight when the Covid-induced crisis demanded the support of the monetary and fiscal policies for its resolution. The MMT is a tight-rope walk and can lead to a lot of collateral damage, with higher inflation being one of them. However, it has substantial benefits as well, so could it be the future? Only time will tell.

For now, let's now take a closer look at the idea of a monetary policy, particularly in an Indian context.

Monetary Policy: The Basics And Its History

Simply put, a monetary policy is a rule book created by a central bank to manage the macroeconomic stability of a country's economy.

The monetary policy of a country, along with its fiscal policy, is something most investors tend to keep an eye on. Let's start with a brief history of India's monetary policy. Up until the 1980s, India followed a socialist model of development, with central planning. The RBI played a supportive role in financing the government's development projects and providing credit to high-priority sectors. Its focus was to lend in a directed manner and control interest rates so that funds could be channelled into the desired sectors, leading to economic growth. The nationalisation of 14 major banks in 1969 expanded the role of the public sector in banking, and increased government control over credit allocation. However, in 1991, in response to a severe balance-of-payments crisis, India initiated economic liberalisation and structural reforms. The RBI shifted its focus from directed lending to a market-oriented monetary policy. The automatic monetisation of the government deficit ended with ad-hoc treasury bills no longer being issued. Thus, the RBI's effective role changed from being a financer for the GOI's plan to containing inflation and promoting growth.

The introduction of the LPG (Liberalisation, Privatisation, Globalisation) reforms led to a gradual dismantling of interest rate controls, as well as the opening up of the financial sector. In 1993, the RBI adopted a multiple-indicator approach, and began using several macroeconomic variables to guide monetary policy decisions. The RBI started using policy instruments such as the repo rate, reverse repo rate, and cash reserve ratio to manage liquidity and influence interest rates. India needed an autonomous central bank, a central bank that would not bend before the government but would instead drive its own operations on the basis of market forces, with an eye towards maintaining price stability and growth.

In 2013, the RBI formally adopted an inflation-targeting framework. The objective of the framework is to maintain price stability while supporting economic growth. The Monetary Policy Committee (MPC), constituted in 2016, became responsible for setting the policy interest rates. The RBI implemented a flexible inflation-targeting regime, with the goal of keeping inflation within a specified range, namely 2-6%, the midpoint of which is 4%. The policy interest rates, such as the repo rate, became the primary tools for influencing inflation and managing monetary conditions. On the growth front, the RBI measures a "potential growth": the growth rate that India can, in principle, sustain given its inputs of labour, capital, and technology, and tries to drive the actual growth closer to the potential growth. For example, if the potential growth rate is 6% and the current growth rate is 2%, the RBI is likely to ease interest rates to support growth.

After 1996, the RBI had to contend with certain new problems because of a change in not only the monetary policy environment but also the exchange rate regime. In February 1993, India had moved to a market-determined exchange rate regime, with intervention by the RBI when needed. Between 1996 and today, India has had to deal with at least three major global exchange market disturbances. The first was the East Asian Crisis, the second the 2008 global financial crisis, including the subsequent taper tantrums in 2013, and the third is the current post-COVID situation. The RBI managed the first two situations with commendable skill, which is also how it's dealing with the third. But one broad lesson is that it is no longer possible to deal with an external situation without also acting on the domestic market dynamics. Therefore, along with growth and price stability considerations, currency also falls within the purview of the RBI.

The Monetary Policy Committee And Its Instruments

So this is what India's monetary policy looks like today. It revolves around 3 factors: price stability, growth support, and curbing exchange-rate volatility. In all, there are 6 members in the Indian Monetary Policy Committee (MPC), with the RBI Governor and Deputy Governor being ex-officio members. The other 4 members are usually nominated for periods of up to 4 years. The MPC is required to meet at least 4 times in a year, though Indian MPC usually meets bi-monthly. The quorum for the meeting of the MPC is 4 members. Each member of the MPC has one vote, and in the event of a deadlock, the Governor has a veto privilege. Moreover, all members of the MPC must write a statement specifying their reasons for voting in favour of or against a proposed resolution.

There are several instruments available to the MPC to help it achieve its objectives of inflation-growth-currency stability, which we will see soon. However, before we dive into that, let's understand a key term related to monetary policy: the liquidity adjustment facility (LAF). The LAF allows banks to borrow funds from the central bank on an overnight basis, using government securities as collateral.

The LAF consists of two components: the repo rate and the reverse repo rate. The repo rate is the rate at which banks can borrow funds from the central bank, while the reverse repo rate is the rate at which banks can park their excess funds with the central bank. Ever since I learned this during my first economics class, I have tried to explain these components in a simpler manner, but the truth is that these definitions need to be memorised and are of extreme importance to understand this chapter any further.

When the central bank wants to inject liquidity into the banking system, it conducts a repo auction, where banks bid for funds by offering government securities as collateral. The central bank provides funds to banks at the repo rate. This infusion of liquidity enables banks to meet their short-term funding requirements.

Conversely, when the central bank wants to absorb liquidity from the system, it conducts a reverse repo auction. Banks can park their excess funds with the central bank and earn interest at the reverse repo rate. This helps the central bank mop up excess liquidity.

The LAF plays a crucial role in regulating the money market rates and ensuring the stability of the banking system. By adjusting the repo and reverse repo rates, the central bank can influence the cost and availability of funds in the banking system, which in turn impacts lending rates, investments, and overall economic activity.

'Interbank liquidity' refers to the availability of funds and the flow of liquidity among banks in the financial system. It represents the ability of banks to borrow and lend money to each other in the interbank market. Banks often need liquidity to meet their short-term funding requirements, manage cash flows, and maintain regulatory requirements. For the longest time, India had a deficit in interbank liquidity which was a conscious policy choice, but since Covid-19 we have maintained a surplus. Surplus liquidity means rate cuts will be effectively transmitted, whereas deficit liquidity means rate hikes will be easily transmitted.

Key Monetary Policy Tools And Techniques

Let's now move on to the definitions of monetary policy instruments:

- **Repo Rate:** The interest rate at which the Reserve Bank provides liquidity under the liquidity adjustment facility (LAF) to all LAF participants against collateral in the form of government-issued and other approved securities.

- **Reverse Repo Rate:** The interest rate at which the Reserve Bank absorbs liquidity from banks against the collateral of eligible government securities under the LAF.

- **Cash Reserve Ratio (CRR):** The average daily balance that a bank is required to maintain with the Reserve Bank as a percentage of its net demand and time liabilities (NDTL). The NDTL is, simply put, the sum of demand deposits (money which is payable when demanded, such as savings accounts) and time deposits (money which is usually payable on maturity, such as fixed deposits). This ratio is close to 4%.

- **Statutory Liquidity Ratio (SLR):** Every bank shall maintain certain percent of its NDTL in risk-free, easy to liquidate instruments such as in the form of unencumbered government securities, cash, and gold. SLR is the ratio of such securities to total assets. This ratio is close to 18%.

- **Marginal Standing Facility (MSF) Rate:** The interest rate at which banks can borrow, on an overnight basis, from the Reserve Bank by dipping into their Statutory Liquidity Ratio (SLR) portfolio up to a predefined limit (2%). The ability of banks to do this provides a safety valve against unanticipated liquidity shocks to the banking system. The MSF rate is set at 25 basis points above the policy repo rate. Think of this as allowing banks to borrow, in extraordinary situations, excess money lying with the RBI!

- **Standing Deposit Facility (SDF) Rate:** This is the rate at which the Reserve Bank accepts uncollateralised deposits, on an overnight basis, from all LAF participants. In addition to its role in liquidity management, the SDF is also a financial stability tool. The SDF rate is set at 25 basis points below the policy repo rate. With the introduction of the SDF in April 2022, the SDF rate replaced the fixed reverse repo rate as the floor of the LAF corridor*. Think of this as allowing banks to park money with the RBI in exceptional situations!

  (*The 'LAF corridor' is a percentage range with the policy repo rate (say 6.5%) at the centre, flanked on either side by the MSF (6.75%) and the SDF (say 6.25%). Thus, the policy corridor has a width of 50 basis points (6.75% - 6.25%).)

- **Main Liquidity Management Tool:** A 14-day-term repo/reverse repo auction is the main liquidity management tool for managing frictional liquidity requirements. In the repo operation, liquidity gets added in the system. In the reverse repo operation, liquidity gets sucked out from the system

- **Fine-Tuning Operations:** The main liquidity operation is supported by fine-tuning operations, carried out overnight and/or over a longer duration, to tide over any unanticipated liquidity changes during the reserve maintenance period. In addition, the Reserve Bank conducts, if needed, longer-term variable-rate repo/reverse repo auctions of more than 14 days.

There are several other methods available to the MPC, such as open market operations (OMOs), where the RBI can buy/sell government securities in the secondary market to affect liquidity. For instance, if the RBI buys securities worth INR 50K, that INR 50K enters the market and gets added to the available liquidity. Given the bond market's dynamics, there is more demand for government securities (i.e. extra demand created by the RBI), and therefore the yields fall or the bonds rally. Thus, OMOs can be used to affect liquidity and bond yields. As one of the RBI's biggest goals is to help the government finance its deficit, OMOs help create demand for government securities and keep the cost of borrowing (yields) lower.

An "undocumented" and very effective tool of monetary policy is the central banks' guidance for the future. Central banks can do a lot just through their commentary.

MPC Meetings And Statements

Now that we're broadly aware of the tools and methods at the disposal of the RBI, let's understand what monetary policy is all about. The MPC typically meets once every two months and takes a holistic overview of the economy, based on their own models, the markets, and professional forecasters. It then decides the ideal interest rate for the economy in the form of cut/hold/pause. It also takes a decision regarding its stance. Historically, there have been 3 stances: hawkish/neutral/dovish. Put simply, the stance reflects the future guidance: a neutral stance indicates a pause on interest rate changes, a hawkish stance creates expectations of a rate increase (and a tightening of liquidity), and a dovish stance creates expectations of falling interest rates (and more liquidity). Post Covid, India has had a new stance — "withdrawal of accommodation" — which indicates higher interest rates but surplus liquidity. Such innovation in the MPC's remarks is always a welcome possibility.

Apart from rates and its stance, the MPC statement contains information on the policy corridor, inflation expectations in the near future, growth expectations in the near future, and other macro variables that may be important at that point. The projections/estimates of growth and inflation serve as benchmarks for future policy decisions. On the day of publication of the MPC statement, the Statement of Development and Regulatory policy is also released; this statement mainly lays out the changes made to the regulations for banks/NBFCs, things like the RTGS timings, UPI with credit cards etc. Twice a year, in April and October, the RBI also releases a Monetary Policy Report which is a very comprehensive overview of the Indian economy and captures its many trends. Thus, the RBI's MPC is very important for the markets and is keenly followed by investors in India and abroad.

A discussion on central banks, however, is not complete without considering a) the money supply and b) their balance sheets

The Money Supply

Perhaps the most important monetary economics equation remains MV = PY. For those of us who have had some exposure to economics, this should definitely ring some bells. The equation basically says that the money supply in the economy can drive growth, i.e. the money supply(M) x velocity of money(V) = price(P) x output(Y) (or nominal GDP)

In fact, for a few years until 1998, the money supply was the intermediate target of the RBI's monetary policy. This state of affairs started to come under question when India started witnessing significant external shocks in the form of capital flows, exchange rate volatility, etc. That's when targeting purely the money supply became difficult, and interest rates started playing a major role. As things stand today, interest rates are the direct target of the Monetary Policy, i.e. the Monetary Policy determines a suitable interest rate based on the its growth and inflation targets. However, lower interest rates indirectly target an increasing money supply or are expansionary in nature. The money supply is a driver of India's growth and inflation, and still a key focus of the RBI's policy action.

M0, also known as narrow money or the monetary base, refers to the most liquid form of money in an economy. It includes physical currency (banknotes and coins) in circulation that's issued by the central bank and commercial banks' deposits with the central bank. For context, in FY22, India's M0 was INR 30 trillion. M0 represents the foundation of the money supply, and is directly controlled by the central bank.

M1 includes a broader range of money than M0. It encompasses M0 and adds demand deposits, which are funds held in checking accounts that are accessible for immediate withdrawal by depositors. It represents the most immediately accessible and widely used forms of money for day-to-day transactions. In FY22, India's M1 was INR 53 trillion.

M2 is an even broader measure of the money supply than M1. It includes all the components of M1 and further adds certain types of near-money or quasi-money. Quasi-money refers to financial assets that are highly liquid and can be easily converted into cash. Examples of quasi-money include savings deposits, money market mutual funds, and other relatively liquid financial instruments. In FY22, India's M2 was INR 54 trillion.

Finally, M3 is the broadest measure of the money supply. It encompasses M2 and then adds to its long-term time deposits, institutional money market funds, and other large and less liquid financial assets. M3 captures a very broad range of financial instruments, and is used to monitor the overall availability of money in an economy. In FY22, India's M3 stood at INR 204 trillion. As these figures indicate, M3 is roughly 5X of M0, so the money multiplier is around 5.

Let's now talk about the velocity of money, which is the nominal GDP (INR 234 trillion for FY22) divided by M3 (INR 204 trillion for FY22).

The velocity of money estimates the pace of movement of the money in an economy — in other words, the number of times the average rupee changes hands over a single year. A high velocity of money indicates a bustling economy with strong economic activity, while a low velocity indicates a general reluctance to spend money.

These measures are essential for enabling policymakers and economists to analyse and monitor the overall liquidity and stability of the financial system. A higher money supply is theoretically said to be inflationary, because there's more money available for a fixed number of goods, leading to an increase in prices. However, all this is very relative, because it depends on other macro factors as well. If productivity goes up along with increase in money supply, the perceived inflationary effects are rather muted.

The Financial Workings Of The RBI

Now, let's move on to the functioning of the RBI and its ability to support the government. It's important to note that the RBI operates with a different objective compared to commercial banks. While commercial banks primarily aim to maximise their profits, the RBI's main focus is to maintain price stability, manage monetary policy, and ensure the stability of the financial system.

The RBI's profits are not distributed to private shareholders but are transferred to the Indian government. The government receives most of the RBI's profits as dividends, which are used to support various public expenditures and fiscal requirements. The news surrounding the RBI's dividends is usually closely followed. The amount of money transferred from the RBI to the central government is determined based on a report constituted by the Bimal Jalan committee. The RBI has several different streams of income and expenditures.

1. **Interest income:** The RBI earns interest income from its investments in government securities, treasury bills, and other approved securities. These investments generate returns in the form of interest payments, which contribute to the RBI's income.

2. **Monetary policy operations:** The RBI conducts monetary policy operations, such as repo and reverse repo auctions, through which it lends money to or borrows money from banks. The interest earned or paid on these operations adds to the RBI's income or expenses. When banks borrow from the RBI, the central bank makes money. When banks park money with the RBI, the central bank pays money.

3. **Foreign exchange operations:** The RBI manages India's foreign exchange reserves and conducts foreign exchange operations to stabilise the value of the Indian rupee. These operations involve buying and selling foreign currencies, and any gains or losses from these transactions contribute to the RBI's income and expenses.

4. **Banking and financial services:** The RBI provides various banking and financial services to commercial banks, the government, and other entities. These services include maintaining

banking accounts, managing the government's debt, and facilitating payments and settlements. The fees and charges levied for these services generate revenue for the RBI.

5. **Surplus from balance sheet:** The RBI's balance sheet includes assets and liabilities, and any surplus generated from its operations contributes to its income. This surplus is calculated by deducting the expenses incurred by the RBI from its total income.

The central bank has certain recurring expenditures, such as the wage bill. Moreover, the RBI must maintain contingency reserves at 5.5%-6.5% of the balance sheet size, and if the reserves go any lower, some money goes out as an expense to add to the reserves. These are just some of the ways in which the RBI's operations affect its profits and losses. Any surplus made after adjusting for these is passed on to the central government as dividends that are used to facilitate fiscal operations.

So at this point, we've already learned a fair bit about our central bank and the monetary policy. This topic can be very deep, and I could go on for a while here (no wonder economics graduates typically have an entire module dedicated to monetary economics!). However, what I'd like to do now is to take a breather and evaluate the effects of the monetary policy on various asset classes.

Monetary Policy And Its Effect On Asset Classes

In the context of commodities: an easier monetary policy, akin to Quantitative Easing in the US (which is when the Federal Reserve buys assets and adds liquidity to the markets), weakens the dollar. The easing of the dollar index can be good for commodities, especially base metals. Essentially, it is assumed that an easier monetary policy leads to higher growth, which leads to higher demand for commodities and therefore higher prices. Also, since globally commodities are priced in dollars, a weaker dollar means higher nominal prices for commodities.

As far as currency is concerned, the easier the monetary policy, the more currency is expected to depreciate. Why? Well, in India's case, for a given dollar amount (assuming no fresh net inflow), there are more rupees entering the economy, which moves the exchange rate upwards, which means that the rupee depreciates. Additionally, money flows better in an economy that has higher interest rates, as investors chase yields. A tighter monetary policy means higher rates, which has a positive impact on currency. And this is why there exists something called the 'central bank's trilemma': lower rates are good for growth, bad for currency, and also bad for inflation, so policymakers always need to consider how much growth can possibly be safely sacrificed. Needless to say, it's a fine balance. In the real world, however, global policymakers usually move together, which means that in terms of the relative picture, the effects of their actions could be muted. For instance, post Covid, in May 2022, the RBI hiked rates a day before the Fed in order to protect the rupee. In other words, because both the US and India did roughly the same thing at the same time, the effect of these actions on the rupee was weaker that it would've been if only one of them had acted in that manner.

For debt market investors, an easier monetary policy is nothing short of bliss, especially when it comes to long-duration debt. Lower the yields, higher the capital gains on bonds. Every action of RBI which has a flavour of expansion- liquidity injection, OMO, outright rate cut etc, benefits debt markets.

Easier monetary policy is also a blessing for equity markets, in general. Lower interest rates typically lead to a lower discount rate used in Discounted Cash Flow (DCF) valuations. A lower discount rate increases the present value of future cash flows, which can positively impact the Price to Earnings Ratio as future earnings are now higher. This is because the lower discount rate reflects a lower cost of capital and implies that future cash flows are worth more in today's rupees. Lower interest rates can reduce the cost of debt for companies. This can lead to lower interest expenses and potentially higher profitability for these companies. Higher profitability can positively affect the valuations. The only caveat here is that easier monetary policy is coming because growth is trending lower, the real earnings of companies could itself take a hit given lower demand scenario, in which case valuation re-rating may get muted. In general, however, higher valuation multiples prevail when interest rates are lower.

With economies becoming more interdependent, understanding monetary policy has become important not only for policymakers and economists but also for citizens. Due to its ability to influence the cost and availability of money, monetary policy has a large role to play in the economic destiny of nations. In addition, a good understanding of monetary policy helps investors make sense of the economic landscape, which can help them make better decisions.

Chapter 7

The Economics Of Commodities: Fair Game Of Demand And Supply

Let's start this chapter by defining what a commodity even is. A commodity is an economic good that is highly or fully fungible, which means that the market considers different instances of such a good as being more or less equivalent, regardless of who produced them.

What this means is that crops, metals, precious stones, mined products, chemicals, etc. are all commodities.

And once you know that, it's clear that the cravings that various civilisations have had over the millennia for various commodities have played a huge role in shaping world history.

For instance, trade relations between India and the Roman empire were so strong in the early centuries of the Common Era that Roman politicians used to bemoan the fact that huge amounts of gold and silver were being lost to India in exchange for silk.

In antiquity, spices were a prized commodity, and the demand for them led to the creation of extensive trade networks. Indeed, in the 15th century, one of the reasons that European explorers set off on perilous journeys was to find new sources of spices. Similarly, one of the motivations that led to the European colonisation of North America was the prospect of growing wealthy from tobacco plantations.

And of course, who can forget the various gold rushes in the 19th century that acted as spurs for the American economy?

More recently, in the 20th century, oil ended up becoming incredibly valuable, with wars being eventually fought over it.

It's not hard to see why commodities are such a big deal: simply put, they're natural resources that are rare but useful. Their trade is an integral part of the global economy, which is why every serious investor needs to be familiar with some of their main characteristics and the impact they have on various markets.

The Fundamentals Of Commodities

Commodity prices are pure demand and supply plays. When demand for a particular commodity exceeds its supply, prices tend to rise, and vice versa. However, commodity cycles are deeply interlinked with all kinds of macro data and all asset classes, and understanding these interconnections is vital.

Let's get started with understanding the fundamentals, which can be applied to most commodities, such as copper, nickel, aluminium, and oil. However, while they're applicable to precious metals to some extent, gold and silver do have some peculiar traits arising from the fact that they're perceived as being low-risk commodities, in contrast to base metals.

As I just said, demand and supply are what matter the most when it comes to commodities. What factors drive demand? The most important factor here is economic growth. When economies are expanding, the demand for commodities is higher. In previous chapters, we have seen measures of industrial performance such as the PMI, factory orders, and the IIP, as well as measures of overall growth such as the GDP. All of these are economic drivers of demand for commodities.

In addition, it's important to know that China is the biggest consumer of most commodities today. The United States, the largest economy in the world by output, comes in second. The growth, industrial performance, and capital expenditure of these economies have a fair amount of bearing on the overall demand for commodities. We have talked quite a bit about policies that can boost growth. For instance, quantitative easing, which involves a central bank purchasing securities and thus introducing money into the economy, does boost the money supply, which is rightly expected to boost growth. Likewise, fiscal expansion, which involves increasing the fiscal deficit due to greater expenditure within the economy, also aids growth. Both monetary and/or fiscal expansion are positive for the demand for commodities, and hence boost commodity prices.

The other demand-related variable for commodities is structural changes. For example, the rise of electric vehicles (EVs) has significant implications for commodity demand, as the transition from traditional internal combustion engine (ICE) vehicles to EVs involves changes in the materials and components used in automotive manufacturing. Now, a higher demand is expected for lithium, nickel, copper, etc. Both structural and short-term factors play a significant role in determining the demand for commodities.

As for the supply of commodities, it can be extrapolated on the basis of the information we have about commodity producers. For instance, if mining companies have carried out more capital expenditure leading to capacity expansion in a given year, then chances are high that the supply of the relevant commodities will increase in the next few years.

As far as oil is concerned, OPEC (the Organisation of the Petroleum Exporting Countries), which consists of a group of oil-producing nations, has historically managed oil production levels so as to influence global oil prices. Historically, OPEC has held regular meetings to discuss and decide on oil supply levels. However, off-late US has become a net exporter of oil and it doesn't form a part of OPEC. Russia isn't a part of it either. Therefore, the effects of OPEC decisions alone can be muted if these giants decide to take a contra call.

When it comes to agricultural commodities, weather changes can be a critical factor: for instance, a flood in a major wheat-exporting country can significantly raise global wheat prices due to buyers anticipating supply shortages. The Russia-Ukraine war not only created expectations of significant supply shortages for oil (as Russia is a major producer) but also for cereals (as Ukraine is a major producer; indeed, it has long been known as the 'breadbasket of Europe').

Such supply squeezes can affect pretty much any commodity, of course. For instance, during Covid-19, a marked semiconductor supply squeeze was created due to factories being shut and global trade slowing down. In sum, supply can be a function of industry trends, business calls by companies, geopolitical events, and several other factors.

A key analytical tool that's paramount to understanding commodity behaviour is something called a commodity curve. A commodity curve, also known as a forward curve or futures curve, represents the relationship between the price of a commodity today and its price in the future at specified delivery dates. Such a curve provides a snapshot of the expected futures prices for a specific commodity at different points in time. Logically, and assuming that nothing else changes, the price of a commodity in the future should be higher than its current price, simply because commodities have a storage cost associated with them. However, the actual curve, i.e. the projected futures prices over a certain time period, may be upward-sloping or downward-sloping, i.e. future prices can be higher or lower.

In a "contango" market, the commodity curve slopes upward, indicating that future prices will be higher than the expected spot prices. Contango curves often occur during periods of ample supply or when the market expects increasing supply levels, which are normal states of affairs. There's no frenzy in the spot markets as traders expect the supply to only get better in the future.

In contrast, in a "backwardation" market, the commodity curve slopes downward, indicating that future prices are expected to be lower than the expected spot prices. Backwardation curves often occur during periods of supply constraints, concerns about future availability, or expectations of increasing demand. Such periods are when there's a frenzy in the spot markets, because there's an expectation that the future is going to be worse than the present, which leads current prices to be higher. This can be because there's a sudden demand spurt in the present or there's an expectation that supply will fall in future.

A backwardation curve is a bullish signal. When a commodity curve is in backwardation, it correlates with high commodity prices in the present time. Correctly interpreting the commodity curve will help investors take a call on commodities. During the 2008 global financial crisis, crude was in sharp backwardation. Similarly, during the first phase of the Russia-Ukraine war, crude went into a sharp backwardation. When one tracks such a curve live and sees it giving up its backwardation, that's when one can assume that the commodity's prices will fall in the near future. Similarly, when one sees a contango curve start to transition into a backwardation curve, one can assume that the commodity's prices will rise in the near future. Thus, commodity curves are among the purest indicators of the markets and their expectations.

Diving In Deeper

Let's now understand a few more drivers of commodity prices.

The Dollar Index (DXY) is an important indicator not just for commodity prices, but also for various other markets. It's a measure of the value of the US dollar relative to a basket of other major currencies. It provides a weighted average of the exchange rates between the US dollar and a group of six currencies: the euro (EUR), Japanese yen (JPY), British pound (GBP), Canadian dollar (CAD), Swedish krona (SEK), and Swiss franc (CHF).

In the last decade, the DXY has moved roughly between 70 and 110, with a reading of 70 meaning a weak dollar and a reading of 110 meaning a very strong dollar. What makes the dollar strong or weak? Simply put, when the US economy is perceived to be stronger than the economies of other countries, the dollar index is strong, and vice versa.

Quantitative easing (QE) in the US is dollar-negative because it introduces more dollars into the economy, leading the dollar to depreciate. An easier monetary policy leads to a weaker currency. In a relative world, money chases higher yields. Therefore, when central banks are in a rate-cutting phase, an economy that has cut down rates relatively more loses inflows. When central banks are in a rate-hiking phase, an economy that has hiked rates relatively more gains inflows.

This is especially true of the two largest developing markets: Europe (the EU) and the USA. When the relative yield of the EU is increasing vis-à-vis US yields, the dollar weakens, and vice versa. Tracking central bank actions is imperative in order to gauge and forecast the movement of the dollar index. In addition, the DXY moves in clear cycles. In fact, the major tops in the dollar are 16 years apart. Therefore, understanding where we are in the DXY's cycle is very important. Lastly, better US data on growth, such as the PMI, retail sales, etc. leads to a stronger dollar. Marrying these indicators with market data such as open interest in the dollar can help us take a call on the dollar.

Commodity prices and the dollar index exhibit an inverse correlation: the stronger the dollar, the lower the commodity prices, and vice versa. Most commodities are traded and priced in US dollars on global commodity exchanges. As a result, when the US dollar gets stronger, it effectively reduces the purchasing power of buyers holding other currencies. This tends to decrease the demand for commodities and puts downward pressure on their prices. Conversely, when the US dollar weakens, it becomes relatively cheaper for foreign buyers to purchase commodities priced in dollars. This increased affordability can stimulate demand for commodities, leading to higher prices. This inverse relationship between commodity prices and the dollar index is an important consideration when it comes to gauging and understanding commodity prices.

Commodity prices can also be studied relative to other asset classes. For instance, a time series (i.e. a data set gathered over a period of time) of an equity-index-to-commodity-index ratio or a bond-index-to-commodity-index ratio can indicate how expensive or cheap commodities are vis-à-vis previous cycles relative to another asset class. This can help identify transitional points in a cycle. A core credo of investing wisdom is that excesses in one direction will lead to excesses in another. Therefore, when an asset class has run out of steam, chances are high that some other asset class will take its place and do well. These ratios allow us to study this theory with hard data.

Let's now understand why precious metals differ somewhat from other commodities. It's true that precious metals are also inversely correlated with the dollar index. It's also true that the demand-supply and commodity curves influence precious metal prices. However, they tend to do even better when economic growth is middling or slowing, and when market players want to reduce their risks. This is because they're considered to be low-risk stores of value. Therefore, the ratio of copper to gold prices can be used to gauge the overall risk sentiment. A higher ratio (i.e. copper prices are on an uptrend) implies a risk-on sentiment, while a lower ratio (i.e. precious metal prices are on an uptrend) implies a risk-off sentiment.

Why Commodity Prices Matter

India is a net importer of commodities, which means that they're an important input variable when it comes to understanding the macroeconomics of the country. As we discussed earlier, commodity prices have a major impact on wholesale price inflation. Commodities are the raw materials in most industries. Higher producer prices will create a push for higher retail prices, due to which higher commodity prices are typically accompanied by higher inflation. As a consequence, higher commodity prices slow down the country's growth, as private consumption suffers.

Additionally, India's imports bill goes up at such times, and we already know higher imports lead to lower output. Higher imports also lead to a higher trade deficit, and worsen our external position. For instance, oil prices increasing by USD 10 per barrel increases our trade deficit by USD 15 billion annually. In the wake of the Covid pandemic, there was a huge surge in commodity prices driven by a supply squeeze, which led to a significant jump in our trade deficit.

On the fiscal front, the dynamics are even more complex. Higher commodity prices do hurt the fiscal situation. When oil prices went sky-high in the aftermath of the Covid pandemic, the Government of India had to reduce excise duties so as to keep pump prices in check, which hurt fiscal revenue. In some cases, subsidies may have to be increased. Either way, higher commodity prices do not help the government budget.

To sum up, India's macros do better when commodity prices are under control. Tracking commodity prices is a must for keeping tabs on and understanding the domestic economy.

Commodities And The Markets

Let's now understand how commodities interact with various other asset classes. Higher commodity prices lead to the depreciation of the currencies of importing countries. The logic is simple: higher commodity prices worsen the trade bill, and cause more dollars to go out of the economy. Due to high commodity prices leading to higher inflation, central banks are expected to hike interest rates, which is bad news for bonds. Therefore, high-duration debt investing benefits from lower commodity prices.

For the equity markets, there's no single convenient analysis. For industries where commodities are the raw materials, a rise in commodity prices creates margin pressures, and is therefore negative for earnings. However, for industries where commodities are the final product, higher commodity prices lead to higher revenues and earnings. It's also true that high commodity prices create pressure in favour of interest rate hikes, which is generally not very positive for equity markets. One needs to weigh the many levels of effects of commodities on companies to deduce the right outcomes for a given situation.

Commodities are the foundation of our global economy. They are the raw materials that are used to produce everything from food and fuel to clothing and electronics. The prices of commodities have a direct impact on our lives, our day-to-day decisions, and our investment portfolios. Governments also take commodity prices into account when making policy decisions.

In recent years, the prices of commodities have been quite volatile. This volatility has been caused by a number of factors, including economic growth, political instability, and climate change. As the world's population continues to grow, the demand for commodities will also keep increasing.

Thus, it's important to understand the role of commodities in the global economy. By doing so, we can make better decisions about our own lives and investments, and can also be in a better position to understand governments' policy decisions.

Chapter 8

Credit: An Economic Lubricant

USD 8 trillion.

That's the staggering amount of wealth that the Global Financial Crisis (GFC) <u>wiped out</u> from US stock markets between late 2007 and 2009. Ordinary Americans fared even worse, as they lost a cumulative USD 9.8 trillion in wealth due falling property prices and emptied-out retirement accounts.

The GFC has, of course, left a rather deep scar on the collective psyche of investors around the world, and has been the subject of extensive research (and of a fantastic film, *The Big Short*) that has tried to bring out the lessons it holds for the future. And if there's one thing we've learnt from all of this analysis, it's that perverting something that's critical to the economy is a recipe for disaster.

What critical aspect of the economy was perverted in the lead-up to the GFC? Credit.

To understand this claim, let's take things from the top.

Home loans in the US typically take the form of mortgages, which simply means that the real estate being purchased serves as collateral in the event of a default. Now, typically, banks vet home loan applicants to make sure that their income is stable enough and large enough for them to pay their mortgages. But in the years leading up to the GFC, several banks relaxed these standards in order to increase their revenue and market share. In other words, they started granting mortgages to people who were at a relatively high risk of default.

In addition, since 2002, banks had been selling securities known as collateralised debt obligations (CDOs), which were basically lots and lots of mortgages of differing risk levels bundled together into a single package.

Why did banks sell these securities? Well, two reasons: they got to offload mortgages (all of which come with some risk of default, no matter how small), and they got an immediate lump-sum payment for the CDO instead of getting loan EMIs over several years or decades.

And why did other entities buy these securities? They perceived them as being low-risk (because they believed that house prices would always keep rising, so even if a small proportion of homeowners defaulted, they could seize their houses and sell them without making a loss), and also as pretty much guaranteed sources of income (thanks to all the monthly EMIs trickling in).

And how did such buyers know that a given CDO didn't have too many risky mortgages in them? Well, CDOs would be vetted and rated by credit rating agencies: a rating of 'AAA', for instance, meant that a CDO was very safe.

Now, at some point, banks started creating CDOs that contained an uncomfortably high proportion of risky mortgages: but only the banks knew that. That's because despite these CDOs' risky nature, banks were able to get reputable credit rating agencies to rate them AAA (due to a variety of factors that we won't get into). And these agencies were so well-regarded that investors would blindly trust them when it came to determining which investments were safe.

Thus, there were two main ways in which the normal process of providing credit was perverted:

1. Lines of credit were extended to people who shouldn't have been given loans, as they didn't really have any way to pay them back.

2. Credit rating agencies failed in their primary duty of accurately and unbiasedly assessing the risk level of securities.

Thus, it turned out that indirectly, the American housing market was built on a foundation of sand. Because when the non-creditworthy homeowners started defaulting in droves, the "guaranteed income" that had been one of the main attractions of CDOs started to dry up. Market players quickly realised that these "subprime" CDOs were far riskier than they'd thought, and worth far less than they'd paid for them.

US markets went into a tizzy, with panic reigning supreme. The stock market crashed. Everyone who had subprime CDOs wanted to get rid of them. The sudden glut in supply tanked their prices and further wiped out the wealth of the institutions that owned them. This sudden loss of wealth shouldn't be underestimated: Lehman Brothers, a well-known financial services firm that was more than 150 years old, ended up going bankrupt as a result of this market rout (as well as other related factors). Its bankruptcy shattered the faith of investors around the world, and caused markets to plummet globally.

The collapse of financial markets meant that market liquidity dried up. As a result, the demand for houses also dropped, causing home prices to fall. This then tanked the net worth of homeowners, which led to even more mortgage defaults!

Things got bad enough that the US government had to step in. However, its first attempt to quell the fire, in the form of the USD 700 billion Emergency Economic Stabilization Act of 2008 (aka the Wall Street bailout), failed to substantially improve the economic situation. It took another stimulus package in the form of the roughly USD 800 billion American Recovery and Reinvestment Act of 2009 to bring some stability to the economy.

The moral of the story? Well, actually, there are several, but one of them is definitely that you can't afford to play fast and loose with certain foundational elements of our modern economic system, lest you bring the whole edifice down on your head. And credit is, without a doubt, one of the most important such core elements: it's an economic grease that keeps things moving smoothly without friction.

The Basics Of Credit

Credit is a major growth stimulator, as it facilitates all the pillars of output: consumption, investment, and trade. It helps whet institutional risk appetite, makes money multiply, and basically helps the economy run itself. Several credit-based indicators are actively tracked in order to derive useful conclusions about the business cycle. The most tracked such indicator? Banking credit.

In the Indian context, this data is captured by the RBI for major scheduled commercial banks, and the complete dataset for a given month is released at the end of the month following it. For example, on 31st of May, the actual banking credit off-take for April will be released.

Before we dive any deeper into understanding banking credit data releases, let's quickly review the process of credit creation. Banks receive deposits from their customers and pay interest on them. For banks, deposits are liabilities. When a bank receives a deposit, it adds a part of the deposited amount to its reserves. This is because all banks have a certain reserve requirement, which is a minimum amount it must always have in its reserves so that it can fulfil depositors' withdrawal demands. Once this reserve requirement has been met, the bank can then create new loans and extend lines of credit to interested parties.

For example, if the reserve requirement is 10% and a bank receives a INR 100 deposit, it can add INR 10 to its reserves and lend out INR 90 as a new loan. Banks earn interest on such loans, and in that sense, credit is an asset for banks. Obviously, the interest rates that banks offer on deposits (say 6%) is lower than the interest rates that banks receive on the loans they give out (say 11%). The difference between these two rates is called the Net Interest Margin (NIM). The higher the NIM of a bank, the greater its profitability.

Another common indicator studied in such contexts is something called the Credit-to-Deposit ratio (or C-D ratio). As the name rather transparently suggests, the C-D ratio is the ratio of the total amount of credit given out to the total amount of deposits received. Theoretically, a higher ratio indicates that the bank is using its deposits to provide higher loans, while a lower ratio suggests a higher level of liquidity and a lower inclination towards loans. Lending is the key business of banks and it is lending that makes them profits.

In practical terms, therefore, this ratio is key when it comes to understanding the risk appetite of the economy. A higher ratio means banks are more willing to take risks, while a lower ratio means banks are okay with sitting on the cash they have rather than lending it out. Thus, during Covid-19, when banks were not very keen on lending, the C-D ratio remained low at 70% (compared to the average of 75%).

Like many things in economics, credit is also a function of demand and supply. Demand can go up when businesses are in expansion mode, a capacity expansion is under way, consumers are buying more assets or spending more via credit cards, etc. Hence, credit demand is high when the economy is in a growth phase; conversely, it's low when growth is low or a crisis has struck, because new activities take a backseat in such situations. Credit supply is high when banks have an incentive to lend, which is typically either that interest rates are high or the quality of borrowers is high.

A major reason for banks reducing their credit supply during bad times is that there's a risk of borrowers not being able to service their debt when the economy is not thriving. During such times, banks can just park the excess money with the RBI and earn interest at the reverse repo rate, which is significantly lower than the loan interest rate but keeps them from having to take any risks. Credit demand and supply eventually leads to actual credit off-take. I believe credit is a concurrent indicator of growth: it does well when economic growth does well.

Credit Data Tracking In India

Now, let's switch back to how all this data is tracked. The banking credit data released by the RBI is available for the following heads:

	Weights in 2023 (rounded up)
Total (1+2)	100.0
1. Food	**0.2**
2. Non-food	**99.9**
2.1) Agriculture and allied activities	*12.5*
2.2) Industry	*24.3*
Micro and small	4.3
Medium	1.9
Large	18.1
2.3) Personal loans	*29.7*
Housing (including priority sector housing)	14.1
Advances against fixed deposits	0.8
Advances to individuals against shares, bonds, etc.	0.1
Outstanding credit card bills	1.5
Education	0.7
Vehicle loans	3.7

	Weights in 2023 (rounded up)
Loans against gold jewellery	0.7
Consumer durables	0.3
Other personal loans	8.1
2.4) Services	**26.4**
Transport operators	1.3
Computer software	0.2
Tourism, hotels, and restaurants	0.5
Professional services	1.0
Shipping	0.1
Aviation	0.2
Trade	6.0
Commercial real estate	2.3
Non-banking financial companies (NBFCs)	9.7
Other services	5.2

Source: RBI

India's total credit book as of 2023 stood at INR 140 trillion; the table above highlights the relative weight for each sector. For instance, personal loans take up 30% of the INR 140 trillion (i.e. about INR 42 trillion). It should be clear that tracking this data can throw light on which parts of the economy are getting a boost. In addition, this data also reflects the effects of some specific policies. For instance, in 2020, the GOI launched the Emergency Credit Line Guarantee Scheme (ECLGS), which essentially enables eligible sectors to get collateral-free loans; ever since then, the credit book for that particular category of loans has, understandably, grown. More specifically, in this particular case, the credit extended to small and medium industries grew. Thus, some effects associated with support policies can be tracked through this data release.

While we've covered all the important aspects of banking credit so far, it should be noted that the total credit in an economy is more than just the banking credit. The RBI periodically issues data measuring the total flow of credit in the economy; the components of this data are as follows:

A. Adjusted non-food banking credit
i) Non-food credit
ii) Non-SLR investment by SCBs
B. Flow from non-banks (B1+B2)
B1. Domestic sources
i) Public and rights issues by non-financial entities
ii) Gross private placements by non-financial entities
iii) Net issuance of CPs subscribed to by non-banks
iv) Net credit by housing finance companies
v) Total accommodation by 4 RBI-regulated AIFIs: NABARD, NHB, SIDBI, and EXIM Bank
vi) Systemically important non-deposit-taking NBFCs and deposit-taking NBFCs (net of banking credit)
vii) LIC's net investment in corporate debt, infrastructure, and social sector
B2. Foreign sources
i) External commercial borrowings / FCCB
ii) ADR/GDR issues excluding banks and financial institutions
iii) Short-term credit from abroad
iv) Foreign direct investment into India
C. Total flow of resources (A+B)

Source: RBI

As we can see, the total credit consists of banking credit as well as credit from other domestic sources, such as public issues, commercial papers (CPs), credit from housing finance companies, credit from the National Bank for Agriculture and Rural Development (NABARD), National Housing Bank (NHB), Small Industries Development Bank of India (SIDBI), and Export-Import Bank of India (EXIM Bank). There's also a component consisting of foreign debt via external commercial borrowings and other debt taken on from abroad. This is the most comprehensive way to understand the total credit situation of the country.

Credit And The Markets

It's overly simplistic to think that one can gain complete insights by trying to study the impact of credit data alone on asset classes. This data usually needs to be studied in concert with a lot of other indicators. Simply put, as far as currencies and commodities are concerned, credit will play the same role as growth, since credit cycles typically run in tandem with business cycles. Additionally, higher credit levels are indicative of greater liquidity and money supply growth, which also aid economic growth.

Debt markets themselves are part of the overall credit landscape, and there are many synergies between them and the credit off-take in the economy. A higher credit off-take leads to a higher money supply, which means that deposits also catch up; with more deposits, banks will have a greater demand for government securities, which will lead to lower yields. At the same time, the bigger money supply resulting from higher credit levels can push both growth and inflation towards the higher end, which can lead to the central bank opting for rate hikes, which push yields up. Thus, studying credit data isn't enough; it needs to be studied in light of the overall macro regime.

Lastly, when it comes to equity markets, tracking credit data by sector can be helpful. For instance, a higher vehicle loan volume is indicative of a growing demand for cars, which has positive repercussions on the auto sector. Similarly, a higher housing loan volume has positive implications for real estate markets. Nevertheless, it should be kept in mind that studying the impact of credit is necessary, but isn't sufficient to provide a comprehensive picture.

Many entrepreneurs would be unable to start a business unless they could take out a loan. Many smart young adults would be unable to improve their career prospects if they couldn't take out an education loan to study abroad. And without vehicle loans and personal loans taken out for weddings, several sectors such as the auto and jewellery sectors would not have been doing as well as they actually are.

The point is that by infusing liquidity into the economy, credit also helps keep the economy chugging along.

The 2008 global financial crisis serves as a stark example of how credit-related issues can lead to a severe economic downturn. It highlights the interconnectedness of financial markets, the importance of responsible lending practices, and the need for effective regulatory frameworks to maintain stability in the financial system.

Chapter 9

The Big Picture: Putting Everything Together

So far, we've covered several key macro indicators in substantial depth. It's now time to tie them all together and understand the power of these indicators in the real world. The insights in this chapter owe a huge debt to my interactions with Sahil Kapoor, a market strategist with more than a decade of experience in the Indian capital markets.

Let's turn the clock back to December 2007. India had had a spectacular bull run between 2002 and 2007. And of course, it was a monthly tradition for traders to get together and spend an evening over drinks and dinner. Every conversation was about capturing multibagger stock ideas. Many traders had extremely categorical views. On being asked about their prognosis for the broader market, their standard response was simply, "It's a bull market". That was that, and nothing else needed to be said. One of the most striking (and discomfiting) aspects of the way some of these traders went about their business was that they would always hold five to seven open long positions in stock futures in addition to being fully invested in equities, and would ride their personal net worth through market-linked ESOPs. Very few of them actually knew what kind of leverage they were sitting on in their personal accounts, especially among those who were allowed to trade markets where they had no positions professionally. There was no dearth of ideas. Each trader could roll his tongue and tell you which multibagger you should be buying in the stock futures market.

A month later, in January 2008, disaster struck in the form of the global financial crisis (GFC). In retrospect, the red flags that should've been identified at that time are very evident. The first and most important was probably the widespread optimism and the belief that every single investor knew exactly what to do. There were investors who had spent barely half a year in the market talking about booking multibagger returns in just a few months, and how 'fundamentals' justified their current multibagger holdings.

Another was the frontline market data, which was clearly asking for a more cautious approach to be adopted. By the time 2007 had ended, Indian equity markets were trading at more than 1x market-cap-to-GDP ratio (see the Annexure for a definition of this and the ratios below), and the price-to-earnings ratio for the Nifty index, which had been ~12x at the start of the bull market in 2002, had more than doubled to 26x by January 2008, an all-time high. Similarly the price-to-book multiple had expanded to more than 4x, one of the highest ratios globally. When earnings momentum was at a peak, Nifty companies were compounding their profits at a 25% CAGR on a rolling 3-year basis. Such was the extent of the bullishness that less than 3% of the top 500 stocks by market cap hit a new 52-week low in the six months preceding the January 2008 peak.

All these indicators coincided with a record 5-year GDP growth CAGR of 8%, excellent credit growth (18% in FY07), and a ferocious pace of tax collection (28% YoY growth in FY07) for the central government. It did appear to be a new era for India. But it was soon made clear that there is no such thing as a new era. The global financial crisis that originated in the United States shook the very foundations of the underlying bullish trend in the Indian economy and markets. One of the channels that impacted the markets the quickest were the flows coming in from foreign institutional investors (FIIs). During the crisis, FIIs, who play a significant role in the Indian stock market, started withdrawing their investments en masse, and putting further investments on hold. This resulted in a sharp decline in foreign capital inflows, negatively impacting the market. FIIs pulled out USD 12 billion between January 2008 and October 2008, the largest outflow that Indian equity markets had ever witnessed in a 10-month period until that point. This record held firm for another 14 years before getting challenged in 2022.

Escalating oil prices caused inflation to remain high, and the global contagion caused liquidity from foreign investors to dry up and confidence among local investors to plummet. This led to the Nifty collapsing by nearly 65% from its peak in 2008 to its low in October of the same year.

Then, the US's unemployment rate, jobless claims numbers, and PMI numbers ended up at new highs while the yield curve collapsed and inverted. This seemed to be the final nail in the coffin for all the claims about there being a structural bull market that participants were so sure about. The commodity curve for base metals had shifted from deep backwardation (a bullish condition) to contango (a bearish condition), indicating that demand-side conditions had already deteriorated. Such an economy wasn't ready to take a financial market shock.

Central Banks And The Power They Wield

Let's zoom out of the Indian situation for a moment and examine matters more broadly. In general, the monetary policy of central banks is of great importance when it comes to arresting financial panics. Take the case of the Panic of 1873, for instance, which was a financial crisis that triggered an economic depression in Europe and North America, and whose effects persisted until 1879 in various parts of the world. Here's an excerpt from the 1873 book 'Lombard Street' by Walter Bagehot:

"Financial panics could be stopped early if the central bank lent freely to solvent firms against good collateral. Put all the money in the window to show depositors there was no need to pull out their cash. If necessary, these loans could be expensive — carrying a 'penalty rate' — to discourage overuse. [...] A panic, in a word, is a species of neuralgia, and according to the rules of science you must not starve it. The holders of the cash reserve must be ready not only to keep it for their own liabilities, but to advance it most freely for the liabilities of others. They must lend to merchants, to minor bankers, to 'this man and that man,' whenever the security is good. In wild periods of alarm, one failure makes many, and the best way to prevent the derivative failures is to arrest the primary failure which causes them". If you ever hear a central bank saying something along these lines, know that the financial crisis raging at the moment will soon be over.

The moral of the story is that it's critical to nip crises in the bud, so that they never get going in the first place, and to strike them in the root if they do get going. The GFC marked the first instance where the US felt compelled to implement massive Quantitative Easing (QE), which involved a huge injection of liquidity. It was difficult to gauge its impact in real time. However, most commentators were in an extreme state of pessimism by then. They argued that QE would be inconsequential because the economic loss was far too deep. The then Federal Reserve Chair Ben Bernanke made a few strong statements such as "The Federal Reserve will continue to explore every potential avenue to improve conditions in credit markets and the broader economy", and also hinted at asset price recovery being positive for the economy and markets. The crisis abated soon after. There are two main lessons here:

1. Extreme pessimism hints at a possible buy call in the market (in other words, buy when nobody else is buying). This is in line with Warren Buffett's famous exhortation to be "fearful when others are greedy, and greedy when others are fearful".

2. When central banks act with full force and conviction, financial crises usually abate, even though a real recovery could take a while. This became evident once again during the 2012 European sovereign debt crisis, as the situation began improving soon after European Central Bank President Mario Draghi delivered a speech now known as the "whatever it takes" speech. Similarly, When the Covid-19 crisis hit, Jerome Powell made a clear statement in March 2020, "We are prepared to use our full range of tools to support the flow of credit to households and business, to help keep the economy strong, and to promote our maximum employment and price stability goals". The markets bottomed out on that very date. So when you see the central bank take decisive action in the midst of a crisis, you might be looking at a golden opportunity, and it might be a good idea to go out with a bucket rather than a thimble.

Parachutes Deployed!

It's fair to say that India's monetary policy wasn't pre-emptive. While the first Fed rate cut happened in late 2007, India delivered its first rate cut only at the fag end of 2008. There was widespread fear among policymakers that the Fed QE would be highly inflationary, and that there was thus a rationale for keeping rates high (9% in October 2008). In most post-recession economic recovery phases, we witness higher levels of inflation. But such inflationary readings are quite normal and have a repetitive pattern across recessions. Key drivers that contribute to this trend are a fall in commodity prices at the beginning of recessions and the rapid recovery which sets in after the bottoming of the business cycle.

For recessions where supply chains are hit, as happened during the Covid-19 pandemic, skyrocketing wholesale prices and input prices cause a spectacular rise in inflation. These fast-moving price trends, while quite painful, are usually relatively short-lived in nature. As supply bottlenecks ease up, prices revert to the mean. The third source of post-recession inflation is the base effect. During a recession, most businesses are unable to raise prices, so they do so once the situation starts to improve. Therefore, instead of fearing inflation, central banks should act aggressively during a crisis to protect growth.

Now, as mentioned above, the GFC began to abate after QE was introduced and the Fed won back the confidence of the markets. It was possible to track the recovery in real time both in the US and in India using the many indicators we have discussed in this book, such as the PMI, IIP, GDP, etc. December 2008, when the PMI stood at 32.4, marked the bottom: a year later, the PMI had soared to 55.9. The US GDP growth bottomed out in Q4 2008 at -8.2%, and had recovered to 3.9% by Q4 2009. Similar signs could be seen in data on non-farm payrolls, retail sales, and credit growth, among many others.

Bonds Vs Equities In And After A Crisis

When a crisis strikes and central banks cut rates, it's bonds that rally first. However, equity typically follows soon after. Why? From the earnings perspective of companies, there are two major costs:

1. Interest costs or the cost of debt (during the entirety of 2009, the Fed's funds rate stood at 0.25% vs the high of 5.25% in August 2007). As central banks cut rates, these costs shrink significantly, leading to higher profits.

2. Commodity costs or raw material costs (crude oil hit a low of USD 39 per barrel in February 2009; compare this to its price of USD 134 per barrel in July 2008). As demand erodes, commodity prices usually correct, and so the cost of raw material falls. The net effect is that company margins eventually improve, which improves profitability and boosts stock prices.

This brings us to another important indicator: the BEER ratio, or the bond equity earnings yield ratio, is a financial indicator used to compare the earnings yield of the stock market to the yield on government bonds. The earnings yield is calculated by taking the inverse of the price-to-earnings (P/E) ratio. It represents the earnings per share divided by the stock price. The yield on a government bond is the annual interest payment divided by the bond price. The BEER ratio is used to assess the relative attractiveness of stocks versus bonds. A higher BEER ratio suggests that bonds may be more attractive than stocks indicating that the stock market may be overvalued. Conversely, a lower BEER ratio may indicate that bonds are less attractive than stocks, indicating that the stock market may be relatively undervalued. Therefore, right after a crisis, when central banks have delivered a rate cut and bonds have rallied, bond yields will typically be low. However, as discussed, equity earnings will have improved, and equity yield will be higher. This makes equity relatively more favourable at the start of the recovery phase.

Limping Back To Normalcy

All cycles are similar. The GFC wasn't all that different either. With the onset of recovery, excesses started to build up again. From a low of 735 in February 2009, the S&P 500 climbed up to 2000 in 2014, delivering a stellar 16% 5-year CAGR. The US GDP was growing at

4% again by late 2013. India's GDP was clocking close to 7%. That's when the Fed decided that QE needed to be reduced. The liquidity-pumping tap had to be throttled. This event and its aftermath are now collectively known as the "taper tantrum". Between December 2013 and July 2014, the Fed reduced its bond purchases by USD 10 billion every month. From bonds being bought up at a fast enough rate to inject USD 85 billion a month, bond purchases were practically brought to zero by the time the event ended. This led to volatility across financial markets.

Europe suffered the most as many of its economies were already weak, especially those of the PIGS nations (Portugal, Italy, Greece, and Spain). Europe was still dealing with the aftermath of the GFC and the European sovereign debt crisis. Many European countries were implementing austerity measures and struggling with high levels of public debt. The taper tantrum increased borrowing costs and added to the economic challenges faced by these countries, further hampering their already-fragile recovery. Some European banks held significant exposure to sovereign debt, especially in countries with weaker fiscal positions. The rise in bond yields during the taper tantrum increased concerns about the solvency of these banks and added pressure to their balance sheets. Additionally, unlike the Federal Reserve's clear communication and coordinated approach during the tapering process, European policymakers faced challenges in coordinating their responses. This lack of a unified response increased market uncertainties and exacerbated the negative impact on European markets. The main lesson from this story is that a strong domestic economy can contain the risk of a global crisis: something we are seeing in India today!

Back in 2013, India's economy wasn't doing great either. After clocking close to 8% growth in 2011, we were back at 4% in 2013. We were also recording double-digit inflation. It was a combination of high global prices plus record-high Minimum Support Prices (MSPs) offered by the government of the time. Secondly, oil prices crossed USD 100 per barrel in 2011 and stayed there for a good two years. Our currency depreciated from 47 INR/USD in FY11 to 62 INR/USD by 2013, resulting in higher imported inflation. This then resulted in high domestic inflation. Consequently, the RBI hiked rates and maintained a liquidity deficit in the system, which took a further toll on our growth. India was battling the twin balance sheet problem: high public debt (the fiscal deficit in FY12 stood at 5.9% of the GDP) and a worsening external situation (a current account deficit of more than 4% in FY12 and FY13). All of this culminated in a volatile equity market.

Oil peaked as demand and supply adjusted: it fell to USD 70 per barrel by Q4 2014 and eased further to USD 50 per barrel in 2015. In September 2013, the RBI announced a special FCNR deposit scheme aimed at bolstering foreign currency reserves and curbing the depreciation of the Indian rupee. Under this scheme, banks were permitted to accept FCNR deposits in major currencies such as the US dollar, euro, British pound, Japanese yen, Canadian dollar, and Australian dollar. The key feature of the 2013 FCNR deposit scheme was that it offered higher interest rates than regular NRI deposits. The scheme had a three-year lock-in period and provided an option for banks to borrow from the RBI against these deposits. Collectively, the swap windows brought in USD 34 billion at a crucial time for India, with USD 26 billion raised through the FCNR route alone. On the fiscal policy front, there was a change in government, and a journey of curtailing the fiscal deficit and controlling inflation started. Together, these factors helped alleviate the Indian economy's woes, and the business cycle improved.

This was then followed by better equity performance. However, this recovery was jittery. Between FY15 and FY18, India went through multiple reforms, with some of the most important ones being: demonetisation, the introduction of the RERA (Real Estate Regulation and Development Act), the NPA (non-performing assets) clean-up, and the introduction of GST (Goods and Services Tax). Each of these was an attack on corruption and had short-term costs. Consumption slowed, and so did corporate profitability. Moreover, the Reserve Bank of India (RBI) adopted a flexible inflation targeting framework in June 2016 with the goal of maintaining price stability and keeping inflation within a specified target range. Under this framework, the RBI set an inflation target of 4% with a tolerance band of +/- 2%. Clearly, there were a lot of policy changes happening at once, and the economy and markets were adjusting. In early 2018, there were clear signs of excesses that were set to revert: all commodity curves were in contango (bearish condition), yield curves had inverted, valuations were at cyclical peaks, and domestic large/mid/small-cap indices went only upwards during all of 2017. The euphoria was back, and how!

Markets Have Their Way To Clear Froth

The party came to a sudden end in late 2018, when the IL&FS (Infrastructure Leasing & Financial Services) crisis came to light. This crisis began when IL&FS, a major infrastructure financing and development company in India, started experiencing severe financial difficulties and defaulting on its debt obligations. The IL&FS crisis triggered a significant liquidity crunch and raised concerns about the overall health of India's non-banking financial sector. The government and regulatory authorities took various measures to address the crisis and restore confidence in the financial system. Equity markets corrected downwards, went up intermittently and then corrected again, giving no significant returns for approximately two years. Due to the major policy changes mentioned above, growth had slowed and lead indicators such as the PMI looked unfavourable.

Another downturn had arrived, but was still somewhat under control. In September 2019, India announced an unprecedented corporate tax cut, which brought back corporate profitability and boosted investor sentiment. On an average, tax rates were brought down by around 10%, depending on factors like the turnover, date of inception, etc. Shaktikanta Das, who was perceived to be market-friendly, was appointed as RBI Governor. India was inching along on a road to recovery...

And then Covid-19 struck! There wasn't much that was different about this crisis, except that this wasn't simply a financial crisis: it was a humanitarian one. It wasn't about being rich or poor, it was about being dead or alive. There were two schools of thought at that time: one that forecast that nothing would ever be the same again, and one that forecast that nothing could beat human resilience. While we know today that the second school prevailed, things could've gone either way. The pandemic tested our convictions with every wave it unleashed. As highlighted before, central banks stood tall, and almost all of them took a "whatever-it-takes" tone. This was in March 2020, which was when markets bottomed out. The financial crisis was over, but the economic crisis continued. All major economic numbers hit new lows during the next few months. India's GDP in Q2 2020 contracted by 23%. Almost every macro indicator was at a record low. Fiscal policy also reasonably stepped up to support the recovery.

However, the post-Covid recovery was slightly different in the sense that the supply squeeze lingered on for longer than usual. One reason for this was that the pandemic kept coming in waves, while another was that the Russia-Ukraine war hampered recovery. Consequently, bonds performed well during the crisis, equities performed well during the recovery phase, and everything else behaved as expected. However, commodity prices remaining elevated was due to the supply squeeze. This led to a more sticky kind of inflation, rather than a purely cyclical one that would've self-corrected within a few quarters. Commodity prices eased when the supply situation had improved.

India's economy was far stronger when Covid-19 came in. Our external vulnerabilities have decreased in number and extent. We now have a conservative financial system with a focus on capital adequacy, a banking sector that doesn't mix with investing and keeps more than enough cushion, an external situation that's being helped by higher service exports, a debt market where FII flows are small and incapable of creating a dent, etc. We have chosen stability over speed. To add to this, all the policies enacted during 2016-2019 have now got past their short-term hiccups, and are ready to yield long-term benefits. Clearly, India is now more resilient in the post-Covid recovery.

10 Things That Always Matter

As we continue to live in the post-Covid recovery phase, here are the main lessons to be learned from taking a top-down view of the markets:

1. Markets always discount (i.e. factor in) future macro data. Markets hit tops and bottoms before the macro data does. Unless the macro data is a major surprise with respect to expectations/consensus/estimates, its release is usually a non-event for the markets. This doesn't mean that macros don't matter, it just means that correctly interpreting them is a valuable skill.

2. Whenever there are excesses in one direction, it's most likely that they will lose steam at some point. While nothing is accurately predictable in advance, typically, an event such as another GFC, a taper tantrum, a policy mistake, or a pandemic, something will usually happen to clear all the froth away. Track data aggressively to know where the excesses lie.

3. The markets didn't care much for policies prior to the 2008 crisis. It was assumed that markets were efficient and would find their way to a balance. Today, after multiple crises and policy interventions, markets expect policies to cushion against shocks. Both monetary and fiscal policies are more important today than before.

4. Markets offer a first-mover advantage to a certain extent. Tracking leading indicators and having conviction in a hypothesis is far more rewarding than switching gears when fresh data is released.

5. The simple part is that it's all cyclical. The complex part is that we'd like to be able to time the cycle. While doing so is possible, it can't be done without understanding the macro regime we're in.

6. Macro regimes are not about this indicator or that, they're about the complete picture. Even if a crisis causes commodity prices to suffer, a case could also be made that the supply squeeze associated with the crisis is bad enough that prices will eventually increase. So it's imperative that you widen your toolkit with more indicators to get a more comprehensive picture.

7. The markets and the nominal GDP do not move together in the short term, and perhaps not even in the long term. Nevertheless, given the large number of ripple effects that economic growth has, it's still vital to keep track of the latter.

8. No single factor can explain any given market. Each market is a complex lattice built out of a confluence of many factors, and it's incredibly hard to make accurate predictions. Like battle-hardened investors, what you should aim to rely on is data-driven and evidence-based tracking, as it produces useful results and could give you the ability to beat the market.

9. A thorough knowledge of the past will give you some insights on when not to be aggressive. Protecting yourself from crises, both monetarily and psychologically, is a never-ending but thoroughly rewarding and satisfying exercise.

10. The only antidote to noise is hard data. If one can contextualise data using market prices, you'll be able to recognise and ignore most of the unnecessary analyses and noise surrounding you.

Chapter 10

Annexure: Speed Course On Major High Frequency Data

The best way to read economic data is to have a mental model that makes it clear which part of the output (private consumption / government consumption / investments / net exports) a given indicator affects. Most indicators are not sufficient on their own, and need to be read together with a bunch of other indicators. However, rigorously tracking these indicators does help us get a holistic overview of the economy. Here's a quick explanation of all the essential indicators and concepts you should be familiar with to get the most out of this book.

All set? Let's go!

Consumption Or Demand Indicators

- **Personal loans:** We already discussed this in the chapter on credit but it is important to note as an important indicator of consumption. Personal loans refer to loans given to individuals, including consumer credit, education loan, loans given for creation/ enhancement of immovable assets (e.g., housing, etc.), and loans given for investment in financial assets (shares, debentures, etc.).

  The data is collected from 40 select scheduled commercial banks, accounting for about 93 per cent of the total non-food credit deployed by all scheduled commercial banks(SCBs). It is sourced from RBI and is updated monthly. Personal loans make up around 29% of Total credit of SCBs, in which housing has a significant contribution of around 14%, followed by vehicle loans.

  Personal loans can stimulate consumer spending, as individuals can use the borrowed funds to add to the demand for goods and services. This increased consumption can contribute to economic growth and expansion in various sectors.

- **Retail payments:** Retail payments are typically all payments between consumers, businesses, and public authorities. Sourced from National Payments Corporation of India(NPCI), it is updated monthly. It is typically a sum total of Debit Transfers and direct debit, Card Payments, Prepaid Payment Instruments and Paper based Instruments. The growth and stability of retail payments indicate the overall purchasing power and confidence of consumers. A higher growth in retail payments is also an indication that use of digital/formal ways of payments are increasing. Tracking of payments via UPI etc is possible with this data set

- **Consumer Sentiment Index:** It measures the outlook towards the economy by households, especially their willingness to spend. It is sourced from Consumer Pyramid Household Survey (CPHS), CMIE and is primarily constructed through sample households from rural and urban areas. It is a set of five questions that give a view of the household's perception with respect to current and prospective household well-being. The higher the sentiment index, the higher is the confidence in the economy.

- **Rural wage growth:** For simplicity, we take the average wage rates of men in rural areas. In reality, data is available across occupations- agriculture, construction etc. This data is sourced from the Labour Bureau, Ministry of Labour and Employment and is updated every month. A significant rise in Rural wage is indicative of Rural recovery. It can also be extrapolated to say companies associated with rural recovery can do better such as some FMCG names, 2-wheelers etc.

- **Non-oil imports:** Non-oil imports make up around 70% of our imports and majorly include engineering, electronic and manufacturing goods. Apart from these, there are imports of chemicals, ores and minerals and agricultural products. The data is sourced from Directorate General of Commercial Intelligence and Statistics and is updated every month. It is a part of the Foreign Trade release. Higher non-oil imports can suggest increased economic activity, rising incomes, and improved consumer confidence. Conversely, a decline in non-oil imports may indicate weaker domestic demand, economic slowdown, or reduced purchasing power.

- **Passenger car sales:** This indicator tracks the domestic sales of passenger cars and is sourced from Society of Indian Automobile Manufacturers (SIAM). It is updated every month. Rising car sales can indicate a strong consumer demand, increased purchasing power, and is usually a phenomenon in good economic cycles. The breakup is available for compact cars, mini cars, SUVs and so on.

- **POL consumption:** It represents the sales of Petroleum products and includes various products including Diesel, LPG, Motor Spirit, Petroleum coke, lubricating oil, with Diesel making almost half of it. The data is sourced from the Ministry of Petroleum and Natural Gas, released in the document PPAC, and is updated every month. This indicator represents the volume of sales by oil companies in the domestic market and therefore is not affected by prices. POL consumption serves as a proxy for energy demand in an economy. Higher POL consumption suggests increased economic activity and industrial production as energy is a crucial input in various sectors such as manufacturing, transportation, and agriculture. Monitoring POL consumption provides insights into the overall health of the economy and can help in assessing the pace of economic growth.

• **Two-wheelers:** Within the domestic sales of two wheelers, motorcycles form the major chunk, with a share of around 62% in the total two-wheeler sales. Other than this, there are scooters, including electric scooters, which has gained major traction, witnessing an increasing share for the past 6-7 years. The data for the same is sourced from the Society and Indian Automobile Manufacturers (SIAM) and is updated every month.

Industry Or Manufacturing Indicators

While we have discussed the most important indicators (PMI, IIP and Eight Core data), let's look at all the other data that is available to us for deeper insights.

- **Credit to industry:** It measures the amount of credit extended to the industrial sector by banks. It reflects the overall lending activity directed towards industrial enterprises, including manufacturing, mining, construction, and other related sectors across micro & small, medium and large enterprises. It can be used to study which part of the industry is doing well. High credit is a function of high credit demand, possibly because expansion is underway or banks are lending at favourable terms. Either way, it concurs with good industrial growth

- **Cement/coal/steel production:** These numbers are available within the Eight Core data release and are updated monthly. They have close linkages with industrial performance and are significant in infrastructure development and construction activities. When an economy is expanding, there is increased demand for infrastructure development, housing construction, and commercial buildings, all of which require these inputs. Increased focus government on capex such as road infrastructure also leads to these numbers doing well

- **Commercial vehicles:** This data is again collected by SIAM and is now available quarterly. The use of commercial vehicles such as trucks, trailers etc is a measure of both auto demand and economic activity

- **Capacity utilisation:** This data is captured by Order Books, Inventories and Capacity Utilisation Survey(OBICUS) which is conducted by Reserve Bank of India. This survey throws light on all 3 parameters- Order books, raw material inventory and capacity utilisation of which capacity utilisation levels is the most tracked indicator. A capacity utilisation number above approximately 75% says that now firms will invest into additional capacity expansion.

Service Sector Indicators

- **Credit to services:** Part of the credit data released monthly, it measures the amount of credit extended to the services sector of an economy. The break-up is available for the sub-sectors such as professional services, aviation, NBFCs and so on. Full components have been covered in the credit chapter

- **Services trade surplus:** India is now becoming a powerhouse for services exports and is expanding its horizon beyond IT services exports alone.

Legal consulting, exports etc are picking up. This indicator is essential to understand exports of services in India

- **Services PMI:** In parallel to Manufacturing PMI discussed in an earlier chapter, services PMI measures the health of the services sector. It is a lead indicator and is available across countries for comparison. A reading above 50 shows expansion and a reading below 50 shows contraction in activity

- **Housing loans:** Higher levels of housing loans indicate higher real estate construction and services activity. The data for the same is obtained from the sectoral deployment of bank credit report of RBI.

- **Airport passenger traffic:** Rising passenger numbers suggest that individuals have the financial capacity and confidence to engage in air travel, signalling a positive economic environment. The data for the same is provided by the Airport Authority of India, Ministry of Civil Aviation and is updated quarterly. It is the measure of mobility of the economy and consumer preferences

- **Railway freight traffic:** It refers to the transportation of goods by railways for which the railway company earns revenue. Commodities transported by railways majorly include coal, followed by iron ore, cement, foodgrain, etc.

The quantity of freight traffic is indicative of the industrial production levels. Industries requiring large amounts of raw materials, such as steel, cement, and manufacturing, heavily rely on railways for transporting their inputs and finished products. This indicator also serves as an indicator of infrastructure development and investment. The Ministry of Railways curates data for the same. However, it is often used to study the services sector since it is a good reflection of transportation services.

- **E-toll collections:** E-toll collections refer to the revenue generated through electronic tolling systems implemented on highways or roads. E-toll collections can serve as a proxy for economic activity in a region or country. When economic activity is robust, there tends to be increased movement of goods and people, resulting in higher traffic volumes and, subsequently, greater toll collections. Conversely, a decline in e-toll collections may indicate a slowdown in economic activity. Areas with significant e-toll collections are likely to be regions experiencing rapid urbanisation, industrial growth, or increased trade. This aggregate can also be indicative of transportation efficiency and congestion levels in a region.

External Sector Indicators

- **Indian rupee (INR/USD):** It reflects the amount of Indian Rupee required to purchase one US dollar and is widely tracked on a daily basis. The data for the same is sourced from Financial Benchmarks India Pvt Ltd and is updated daily. The exchange rate is affected by various macroeconomic factors such as Interest rate, GDP, Inflation and foreign flows.

  India has been following a managed floating exchange rate regime. This means that the exchange rate is determined by market forces, but the central bank (RBI) can intervene in the market to buy or sell foreign currency in order to smooth out fluctuations in the exchange rate.

- **REER:** The real effective exchange rate (REER) compares a nation's currency value against the weighted average of the currencies of its major trading partners. It is an indicator of the international competitiveness of a nation in comparison with its trade partners. The data for the same is sourced from RBI and is updated monthly. An increase in the REER implies that exports become more expensive and imports become cheaper; therefore, an increase indicates a loss in trade competitiveness. The REER is adjusted for the effects of inflation for every currency in the basket, enabling it to be a measure of what can actually be purchased by a currency. The REER is used to understand how well a currency is doing with respect to other currencies and also with respect to itself in the past. An REER above 100 shows a currency's strength and overvaluation, and one below 100 indicates a weak currency. A very high REER points at possible depreciation and very low REER points at possible appreciation

- **6-month forward premium of USD:** The 6-month forward premium of USD is a macroeconomic indicator that provides insight into the expected future value of the U.S. dollar relative to other currencies over a 6-month period. The forward premium or forward discount is the percentage difference between the forward exchange rate and the spot exchange rate (the current exchange rate at the time of the transaction). If the forward exchange rate is higher than the spot exchange rate, it implies a forward premium, and if it is lower, it indicates a forward discount. The data for the same is taken from RBI and is updated daily.

- **FX reserves USD Bn:** It reflects the amount of foreign currency held by a country's central bank. It represents the stockpile of foreign currencies, primarily in US dollars (USD), that a country can use to stabilise its domestic currency, intervene in foreign exchange markets, and meet international payment obligations. Total FX Reserves = Foreign currency assets + Gold + Special Drawing Rights (SDRs) + Reserve Tranche position in IMF, with all these values in USD Bn. The data is collected from RBI and is updated weekly. Monitoring the level and trend of a country's FX reserves is important for policymakers, economists, and investors to assess a nation's external financial position and economic stability. Sudden declines or insufficient reserves can indicate vulnerabilities in a country's economy, such as potential currency crises, liquidity shortages, or difficulties in meeting international obligations.

- **Trade balance:** It measures the difference between a country's exports and imports of goods and services over a specified period and is available to track every month. It provides valuable insights into a country's international trade performance and the flow of goods and services across its borders.A positive trade balance, often referred to as a trade surplus, occurs when a country's exports exceed its imports. Conversely, a negative trade balance, known as a trade deficit, arises when a country's imports surpass its exports. More details have been discussed in the chapter.

- **Crude Indian basket:** The Indian basket of crude oil represents a derived basket comprising Sour grade (Oman & Dubai average) and Sweet grade (Brent Dated) of Crude oil processed in Indian refineries. The data is available on a daily basis. This indicator is most relevant to track the global crude prices in the Indian context.

- **Current account balance:** Again covered in much detail in the chapter, it measures the imbalance between a country's dollar inflows and outflows, including trade of goods and services, private transfers, and net income from abroad. It is available quarterly. By expressing the CAD as a percentage of GDP, we can evaluate the significance of the deficit in relation to the country's economic size and indulge in cross-country comparison.

Monetary Indicators

- **M3 (broad money):** M3 represents the broadest measure of money supply within the economy. M3 provides a comprehensive view of the money supply. An increase in M3 may indicate strong demand for credit and investment, co-existing with economic expansion. Conversely, a decline in M3 growth may indicate a slowdown in lending and economic activity.

- **M3/M0:** Also known as money multiplier, the ratio of M3 to M0 is a measure of how much money multiplies in an economy. It provides insights into the extent to which the broader money supply expands beyond the base money provided by the central bank. A higher M3/M0 ratio indicates a higher level of money creation and expansion by the banking system through lending and deposit creation. The M3/M0 ratio is often used to assess the level of financial intermediation and credit creation in an economy.

- **Gsec 10-year yield:** This indicator reflects the Yield on 10 Year Residual Maturity of Government of India dated Securities in Secondary Market. We note here that Government securities are almost risk-free assets. It serves as a benchmark for borrowing costs, reflecting changes in interest rates for mortgages, corporate loans, and consumer loans. Additionally, it provides insights into inflation and growth expectations, with increasing yields indicating higher inflation expectations and improving growth outlook. It also provides central banks a tool for measuring transmission- if yields rise too quickly, it can indicate tightening financial conditions, making borrowing more expensive for businesses and consumers. Central banks may adjust their policies, such as increasing or decreasing interest rates, to manage the impact on the broader economy.

- **5-year AAA yield:** These are the weighted average of yields of 5-year AAA rates companies. 5-years tends to be one of the liquid papers in corporate bond markets and therefore this yield is a good gauge of activity in the corporate bond market. 5-Year AAA Yield reflects the prevailing market sentiment and risk perception. When investors have confidence in the economy and expect low default risk, the yield tends to be lower. Conversely, during periods of economic uncertainty or high-risk perception, the yield tends to be higher. When central banks implement expansionary monetary policies, such as lowering interest rates or engaging in quantitative easing, it can help yields move downwards. Conversely, tightening monetary policy can lead to higher yields as borrowing becomes more expensive. The difference between corporate yield and Gsec yield is the 'risk premium', i.e, higher yield is commanded because companies can default but Government debt is risk free.

- **5-year AA yield:** It is the yield in the secondary market of 5-Year residual maturity AA rated corporate bonds. As the credit rating increases, the risk of default decreases, leading to lower yields because investors are willing to accept lower returns for safer investments. Therefore, usually AAA yields are lower than AA yields.

- **Credit-to-deposit ratio:** It measures the proportion of a country's bank deposits that are being used to extend credit or loans. It is calculated by dividing the total amount of credit outstanding in the economy by the total amount of deposits held by banks. Also, provides an understanding of the lending activity and liquidity position of banks within an economy. A high credit-to-deposit ratio implies that a larger proportion of deposits is being utilised for lending purposes. This means that there is both demand and supply of credit in the economy.

Fiscal Indicators

While we spoke in detail on fiscal indicators, especially in the context of the union budget, there are quite a few of them that can be tracked monthly. The monthly tracking helps us to gauge the path that the economy is treading on and estimate the probability of budget expectations coming true.

- **Revenue expenditure:** It is the expenditure incurred by the government on recurring activities such as allocation to certain schemes, wages and pensions, subsidies, and other operating expenses of the government. A significant portion of revenue expenditure also includes interest payments. Data for the same is supplied by the Ministry of Finance and is updated monthly. One can track this data monthly to see the quantum of government expenditure as well as the relevant economic activities where money is being spent on.

- **Capital expenditure:** Central government's capital expenditure refers to the amount of money spent by the central government on acquiring or creating physical assets, such as infrastructure projects, public buildings, transportation systems, and other long-term investments. The level and allocation of capital expenditure reflect the government's priorities. Again, tracking this monthly helps to understand which part of the economy (roads/ railways/power/ defence etc) is getting government support. Some of it can also be extrapolated to study investment opportunities in these sectors

- **Total expenditure:** It is the sum total of revenue and capital expenditure. Central government expenditure has significant implications for the overall economy and plays a role in influencing aggregate output. It can, thus, stimulate economic growth and stabilise the economy during periods of low activity. However, excessive spending beyond the capacity of the economy to produce goods and services can lead to inflationary pressures. Conversely, insufficient spending may result in sluggish economic growth or even recession. The bigger use case is to study this data monthly and estimate if the government is on track to meet its budget targets. If not, what can be the possible repercussions? For instance, if the expenditure in the first six months has been higher it means either the expenditure will be lower in the next 6 months or the government will have to borrow more.

- **Total receipt:** It refers to the total amount of income generated by the government through all channels. Again, tracking this data monthly helps to estimate if government's revenues are on track. Tax collections are also an indicator of buoyancy in economic activity. Higher tax collected implies that economic activity is progressing well.

- **E-way bills:** E-way bills are electronic documents required for the movement of goods in India under the Goods and Services Tax (GST) regime. They serve as a tracking mechanism for the transportation of goods. E-way bills can be used to gauge the movement of goods, level of trade and economic activity. An increase in e-way bill generation indicates a higher volume of goods being transported. E-way bills are directly linked to the GST system, which is a major source of tax revenue for the government. Monitoring e-way bill generation can help assess the overall tax collection trends, providing insights into government revenue and fiscal health. The data is obtained from the GST Network.

- **Goods and services tax:** GST is a consumption-based tax levied on the supply of goods and services, replacing multiple indirect taxes. Higher collections indicate increased economic activity, consumption, and tax compliance. GST data often makes it to newspaper headlines to indicate economic activity. The data is sourced from the GST council.

Flows In Markets And Economy

This is a set of data that can be tracked to understand the foreign money coming into our markets/economy. Just like Foreign Institutional Investors(FII) flows, Domestic Institutional Flows' data can be tracked too

- **FII net debt:** This measures investment in Debt by Foreign Institutional Investor is sourced from the CDSL and is updated daily. When FIIs invest in debt instruments such as government bonds or corporate bonds, it brings in foreign capital, which can impact the exchange rate of the domestic currency and also contributes to market liquidity. As a matter of fact, FIIs have not exhausted limits on domestic debt off-late

- **FII (Foreign Institutional Investors) net equity:** FII investment in equity represents foreign capital inflows into the country's financial markets. The data is sourced from the CDSL and is updated daily. FII investment in equity is often considered an indicator of a country's economic potential.

Robust FII inflows suggest that foreign investors perceive the country as an attractive investment destination. Such investment boosts a country's foreign exchange reserves. As FIIs invest in equity, they typically purchase domestic currency to make the investment. This can increase the country's foreign exchange reserves, especially if the investment inflows are significant.

- **Net FDI (Foreign Direct Equity) flows:** Unlike FII investment flows, FDIs are not about owning financial instruments of a company but about owning a significant share of the company via vehicles such as joint ventures and strategic alliances. Net FDI Flows are calculated by subtracting Foreign Direct Investment by India from Foreign Direct Investment to India, across various sectors. Although manufacturing FDI is beginning to pick pace, the largest share of FDI is committed to services like Banking and Insurance. The data for Net FDI is sourced from RBI and is updated monthly. Net FDI is often seen as a driver of economic growth and development as it brings in capital, technology, managerial expertise, and access to global markets. Monitoring net FDI trends allows policymakers to identify sectors that are attracting significant investment and those that require policy support.

- **Private transfers:** Net inflows to and from abroad in the form of remittances, gifts, inheritance and support payments is generally referred to as private transfers. For instance, if my cousin working in the US sends money to his family in India, it will be accounted for as a private transfer. Inflows of private transfers, such as remittances, are recorded as current account receipts and are a source of foreign exchange earnings for the receiving country. The data is sourced from RBI and is updated every quarter.

- **ECBs (External Commercial Borrowings):** ECBs refer to commercial loans in the form of bank loans, securitized instruments, buyers' credit, suppliers' credit availed of from non-resident lenders. The data is sourced from RBI and is updated every quarter. ECBs impact the exchange rate and external debt dynamics of a country. Large inflows of ECBs can lead to an increase in the demand for domestic currency, potentially strengthening the currency's value.

These flows are mostly foreign flows. Additionally, there are domestic flows as well such as the money DIIs (Domestic Institutional Investors) are putting in domestic markets. Also, SIP(Systematic Investment Plans) have grown big and that book also brings in substantial flows to the markets. All of these are crucial to understand the flows in markets.

Equity Valuation Indicators

There are multiple ways to value equity markets and there's no one way which is enough. A holistic picture is necessary. Here are some of the most tracked valuation indicators:

- **Market-cap-to-GDP:** The market capitalization-to-GDP ratio, also known as the Buffett Indicator, is a metric used to assess the overall valuation of a country's stock market relative to its gross domestic product (GDP). The idea is that if the market cap is much higher than GDP then it is unsustainable and is likely to correct. Lower ratio implies markets can move up. Advanced economies sustainably have higher ratios because listed space depicts a bigger portion of the economy

- **Price-to-earnings:** It is calculated by dividing the market price per share of a stock by its earnings per share (EPS). The P/E ratio provides insight into how much investors are willing to pay for each dollar of a company's earnings. A high P/E ratio suggests that investors have high expectations for the company's future growth and are willing to pay a premium for its stock. Conversely, a low P/E ratio may indicate that the stock is undervalued or that investors have lower expectations for the company's future performance. It's important to note that P/E ratios vary across industries and sectors, so it's typically more meaningful to compare the P/E ratio of a company with its peers in the same industry

- **Price-to-book:** The price-to-book (P/B) ratio is a financial metric used to assess the valuation of a company's stock relative to its book value. It is calculated by dividing the market price per share of a stock by its book value per share.The book value of a company is determined by subtracting its total liabilities from its total assets, and then dividing the result by the number of outstanding shares. The book value represents the net worth of a company on its balance sheet. It has the same interpretations as P/E and is commonly used for banking, IT sectors.

Note: While this annexure is not meant to be an exhaustive list of all the terminology that might prove useful when reading this book, it does contain all the most important indicators that one can track to widen their investing toolkit.

10 Statements That Are Best Ignored

1. "Macros are not important for Indian markets"

2. "Markets always give nominal GDP returns in long term"

3. "I only listen to macros to sound smart in front of audience"

4. "So which stock should I invest in"

5. "But economists don't make money"

6. "Economics work in Developed Markets, Not India"

7. "You can ignore policy if you're a good stock-picker'

8. "What's your 5-year forecast?"

9. "Markets always react to macroeconomics data in the same way"

10. "All similar cycles have same macros at play"